# Surrender, Submit, Serve Her.

The definitive guide
Leadership and embracing the Female
Dominated Household

**Title**: Surrender, Submit, Serve Her: The definitive guide to enacting Female Leadership and embracing the Female Dominated Household.

**Author**: Key Barrett, MSc

**Pub Date**: 1st edition Jan, 2017

**ISBN**: 9781520203263

## About the Author

Key Barrett is the pseudonym of a published author. What is not a pseudonym is the M.Sc. He has a Masters of Science in Anthropology. Key has studied sexual subcultures across to Europe and North America. He has legally investigated a diverse set of subcultures spanning from female sexual dynamism and aggression in medieval European texts to the bondage and submission clubs of New York to the transsexual burlesque cultures of the Deep South.

## Disclaimer

This book is intended as a marital aid. It is meant to assist couples seeking to embrace a Female dominant lifestyle. It is NOT absolute and is not intended to be used in lieu of couples therapy. Use the suggestions in this book at your own discretion. The author makes no claims that the ideas contained in this book will work for you. He hopes they will.

# Foreword

This is not secretly a book about sex. There are no pictures in this book. There aren't even any illustrations. Yes, there is a whole section at the end devoted to it and this book will indeed touch on sex in a female dominant lifestyle. You can skip forward to that section if you want but I wouldn't recommend it.

You need to understand now (whether you be hopeful male or hopeful female) this book is a serious one. Not that sex isn't a serious topic, but before you get to the sex you will go through the myriad aspects of everyday life that can constrict or enrich your bedroom adventures.

This book takes the idea of a woman led household (a term referred to here as *Female Leadership)* most seriously. Sex is the payoff for both the male soldier and the female commander, but to really enjoy it you must first understand and then commit to the grunt work that makes an army run. Being subservient in bed and a selfish asshole on everything else it takes to run a complete household is not submission to Female Leadership, it's just being a prick. So if that's what you want, best you put this book down now.

On the female side, hoping you can get a man to submit to your leadership because you dominate him in bed isn't rewarding him, it's being a horrible leader. A good leader learns the strengths and weaknesses of their retinue. Don't punish failure, recognize it for the opportunity to train a neophyte exactly as you would want them to be.

Failure is a great opportunity, because you don't have to un-train anything (which is the hardest thing to do). Instead, it's an opportunity to get it precisely as you want (and with men, being exact in description matters). Being forceful and direct in your needs will never be considered 'nagging'. I abhor that term, because what is nagging if not the directions of a dominant woman processed through a sexist and patriarchal system? No person on either side of nagging likes it.

So there you go. If you are ready on the male side to learn all the unglamorous, unsexy aspects of being the household Sergeant-at-arms for your Mistress, and if on the female side, you are willing to stop using sex as a weapon or a reward, and trust in your instinct and be direct with your man, damn his feelings, then this book is for you. The bonus being, at the end, you do get to the naughty (always intimate) sexy bits.
Good luck.

## Who is This Book For?

Men and Women (or women and women) over the age of 18 who wish to establish a household with the woman in charge. If you are looking to understand the benefits and reasons for *Female Leadership* as a way of life, as well as how to implement female control in your household, this book is for you.

## Book Structure

This book is broken into three parts:

- **Surrender** - surrendering to the idea of female leadership.
- **Submit** - submitting to a female leader and learning to live and thrive in a female-led household.
- **Serve** - serving the female leader.

Along the way there are tips and reminders to help absorb the most important takeaways from each section.

**Tips** and **Reminders** take this form.

There are examples of both working Female led relationships and problems within relationships both

Female led and otherwise. Note: The people and relationships are made up for the purpose of this book.

*Kara and Andrew* - examples take this form.

At the end there is a glossary of terms used throughout the book.


## How to Read This Book

This book is intended to be read aloud. This can either be done by the man who hopes to serve or the Woman who hopes to lead. What should happen, no matter who reads it aloud, is that the Female leader should feel free to stop at any point in order to discuss points of contention or agreement. It's crucial that She feel confident to stop and say 'That doesn't work for me', or 'I don't want that' or even 'This is what I've been trying to explain but couldn't'. Don't worry about offending me, I can take it.

This book is meant to be a guide and a set of tools for you but not an end-all be-all. No relationship is one-size-fits-all so you shouldn't expect that everything in here will fit your needs or be something you like. It is of major importance that the Female leader feel free to voice Her concerns and agreements at any time along the way. It is better to catch disagreements with the text early rather than later.

> **Remember -** She has the right and should feel comfortable to stop the reading at any time to voice concerns, disagree with or otherwise discuss what was just read.

Though this book is meant for both Female leaders and male followers, the book is written mainly from the perspective of teaching the male how to serve the Female. This is just a practical way of writing it. Mostly, the Female knows how to lead since it's a quality She is born into and also, there is much more to teaching a man to serve than teaching a Woman to lead.

# INTRODUCTION

"When She first suggested it I laughed, who wouldn't? She laughed too, but She brought it up again later that week. By the 4th time She brought it up I was willing to at least listen to it. I was very resistant to the idea. It all seemed so stupid, this idea my girlfriend had some 'natural authority' over me. But then I recited the pledge to Her. She had me repeat it until the giggles were gone and I was focused on Her. At that moment it made total sense to me. It was natural after all."

First, the bad news - This book is probably only going to apply to about 10 or 15% of the population. A lot of women simply don't want to be leaders of their household or at work. A lot of men don't want to be foot soldiers. But just as there are a certain percentage of men who want to be leaders, so too, there are women in equal numbers who want to lead just as much as men do.

In fact women are natural born leaders. Mothers even more so. But they are susceptible to second-guessing and gas lighting and this keeps many strong women from leading.

This is a holdover from the Victorian society that sold female sexuality as threatening and female power even more so. Victorian men were terrified of female power, which is why they dressed their women in constricting whalebone corsets, reversed property laws, and criminalized sex.

Even the female orgasm was labelled a myth and the 'symptoms' of a female orgasm were labelled 'histrionics' (Hysterika being Greek for the uterus) in need of psychological intervention. The simple truth is some of the strongest and longest lasting rulers in the western Hemisphere have been Women: Queen Victoria (Ironic, isn't it?), Queen Beatrix of the Netherlands, Queen Elizabeth Tudor, etc. And She ain't called Catherine the 'average'. She's Catherine the great, fabled for Her leadership AND Her sexual prowess.

Of course, sexism and male panic didn't stop when Queen Victoria died. It continued unabated through the 20th century and on to today. One need only look at your average Disney film to see how we indoctrinate our youth to the visual queues for threatening female sexuality and the 'joys' of female submissiveness. Almost every fairy tale from the mouse pits a raven-haired evil woman dressed like a dominatrix against a perfect princess in a mortal battle over the male ideal milquetoast.

This villainous ideal of a witch/dominatrix seeks to put Female leadership in a bad light. It teaches our kids not so subtlety that a woman who seeks to control men the way men control women is a perversion of nature. This perversion hypersexualizes Her, exaggerating Her features and Her voice. Most of the time Her female power and overt eroticism corrupts nature itself. Her hideout is always in the midst of some dark and thorny woods.

These Disney dominas almost always have singular goals: Humiliating the men in general and capturing and enslaving the prince. If you're reading sexual enslavement into that, you're right. It's a slander and attempt to cast Female Leadership as something that will enslave all men and turn Good Girls Bad.

The powerful woman seeks to emasculate the man, while the pert, perky princess with the light hair, vacant doe eyes and nice but not too overstated sexual features seeks to raise a family and start a happy life of motherhood and submissiveness. This is the societal programming that most of you have and seek to undo.

---

**Tip!** - Society indoctrinates you from a young age to believe Female Leadership is dangerous and against nature. Work to deprogram these thoughts and keep an eye out for when media is telling you.

---

On a personal aside, I don't know about you but it always seems like Prince Philip ultimately wanted to lose the battle against Maleficent. She's intriguing, stunning, and far more interesting a person then Sleeping Beauty. Her leadership and Her promise of adventures both physical and psychosexual would pose a challenge to Philip that would fall outside the norms of being just another prince. Like many people forced into leadership, he might actually find the submissive role liberating. What a great pair they might have made. Oh well.

So, I guess in the end if you kind of found yourselves rooting for Maleficent then this book is for you. You both have an interesting, challenging, fun and sexy journey ahead and Bonus! You've already got your Halloween costumes laid out.

Now the good news - if you're both reading this book that means this book is for you. Likely in some form or another the Wife has been taking a commanding role in the dynamic already. This book will help you iron out the issues that stand in the way of enjoying each other in your newfound roles.

# For Her

These chapters are not meant to be read alone, that is they don't have to be. In fact reading the whole book together is ideal. It allows you to discuss what appeals to you and what doesn't in a safe and healthy way. This book is not an all-or-nothing proposition. No one household dynamic is exactly like another. Think instead of this book as a box of tools that will help you craft your female led household and you can pick and choose which tools work the best in forging the ideal pairing.

So the first question should be 'What do you hope to get out of this'? here are some good options:

- Greater satisfaction in a relationship.

- Lower stress levels.
- Decreased arguments, decreased misunderstanding.
- A smoother running household in less time.
- Greater sexual satisfaction and excitement.
- Greater sense of self and of your value.
- More confidence.
- Deeper respect for your partner.
- Deeper sense of purpose.
- More successful work life.

This is not an exhaustive list but it's a good start on the way to considering what you really want in a Female Led Household.

## What are the Risks?

What you need to understand about accepting your husband's servitude and taking on the responsibility of being his leader is that he is making an incredible sacrifice and taking a big gamble agreeing to this. This doesn't mean he doesn't want it just as much or perhaps even more than you want it. But he is placing himself under your authority and this carries with it a great and fairly one-sided risk.

He will have great fears about his masculinity and how you now see him. He is agreeing to be vulnerable to you in order to serve your agenda and prop you up as a great leader. There is certainly a lot of trust required with that.

He is trusting that you understand that being a submissive is not the same as being a slave.

There will be resistance at times from him. Especially early. Your authority will be questioned. You will want to fall back into old routines, so will he. But with high risk comes high reward. Be patient. And use the tools (especially reinforcing commitment with judicious use of the pledge) to bring everything back in line. And of course, use patience and understanding. This is a hard change. But it's well worth it.

## For Him

Where to begin? Well, if you're using this book the way I've suggested, you just heard your Wife or partner read out Her section. What did it feel like to hear those words? What went through your head when you were described as vulnerable and submissive? It should have made you nervous and excited, and if your pride and machismo bristled at it a bit, that's okay and normal. It will again.

And it's not supposed to die or go away, either. You're just gonna retool it in a more useful way. But we will get to that. Let's focus on the beginning. So you're considering taking on the role of second-in-command to your fantastic General-in-waiting, eh? Well, what should you hope to get out of this?

- A better understanding of your Wife's needs and desires and how to fulfill them!
- Greatly reduced stress levels.
- Breaking free of masculine expectation while feeling more like a man than you ever had.
- Greater sense of purpose and direction.
- Greater value of your manhood and worth.
- Better emotional and sexual connection to your Wife.
- Increased skills and abilities.
- A more rounded personality.

So hopefully you are both excited to make the change and embrace Her natural wonderful Female Leadership and all the benefits to your household that comes with it. But, what does *Female Leadership* even mean?

# WHAT IS *FEMALE LEADERSHIP?*

"I cannot tell you what it was like that first week. I was so scared. What if I failed? What if I wasn't a good leader? I wanted this, but if it didn't work out, what would that mean? Would he divorce me? Of course, we failed a bunch that first week. I slipped to the old ways, so did he. But when we sat down for our weekly meeting I realized halfway through that my husband was sitting attentively, just listening to me. Not waiting for his turn to speak, not offering advice, just listening patiently and paying attention to what I wanted done and **how I wanted it done.** From that moment on I was a leader, because I had a great follower."

- Sela, leader of Her household since 2009.

14

*Female Leadership* is a structure in which the household is built around the control and direction of the dominant woman in the house. Simply put, She runs the show and you support Her decisions through action. She is the queen of the household. This is more than the house. Her judgement is paramount to the success of all aspects of the family life.

Everyone in the house has abdicated the role of final decision maker and arbiter to Her. This cannot be done out of fear. It has to come from a place of belief and trust. The hopes of the husband is that placing responsibility and authority in the hands of the Wife will bring about harmony and a smoother, more efficient household, marital relationship and sexual life.

A *Female Dominant Household* will be different from house to house but will always have certain characteristics:

- A well maintained and organized house. Under the auspices of a great Female Leader, tasks are delegated fairly and built around tried and true

15

processes. She explains and guides Her subordinate on the proper way to do those tasks, leading to less misunderstanding and greater satisfaction in work.

- A clear understanding of 'Her Way'. The husband abdicates controlling the narrative on how things should be done and agrees to please his Female Leader by not only accomplishing tasks but accomplishing them in the fashion She desires, even if there may be different acceptable ways to do it. The goal isn't to just get something done, but to finish it in a way that doesn't require 'policing' or the dreaded nagging.

- A balanced budget. Female leadership won't make you rich, but it will reduce greatly the stress of money. The husband may often be the one tasked with handling bills and the budget, with the underlying understanding that on all matters of expense, Her word is the **final** word.

- A strong feeling of connectedness. Often relationships suffer because couples retain a large sense of individualism, which leads to conflict. I characterize those marriages as roommates with benefits. That is less than ideal and doesn't last. The Female Dominant Household is one filled with trust, and two people depending on the other to allow them to work towards their strengths. When in harmony, the relationship seems like a real 'We', as opposed to 'She and I' or 'me'.

- A rich and deeply satisfying sex life. There will be a greater emotional sexual connection, filled with deep and unique experiences, experiences guided by the direction of the Female Leader. The emotional connection forged by the vulnerability that comes from male surrender, combined with the Female Leader's sense of well-being derived from Her successful leadership of the household will lead to interconnectedness, experimentation, and immensely pleasurable intimacy.

---

**Remember!** She runs the show and you support Her decisions through your actions.

---

## A few working examples

*Alexandra and Michael*

Six months ago Michael accepted Alexandra's authority over their household and has constantly worked to improve for Her. There have been ups and downs but mostly ups. Both are happier than they have ever been in their relationship and life in general. One of the consequences of Alexandra's leadership has been an increase in savings. Michael wants to spend the 1,500 dollars on a new television, whereas Alexandra wants to put it towards paying off the car.

Alexandra wants to reward Michael for the hard work and agrees that they can get a new tv, but the 600 dollar one. The rest will go towards the car. Because Michael accepts Her authority as implicit, Alexandra's word on the matter is final. Michael is happy that She felt like rewarding him, and he recognizes Her leadership has resulted in a better outcome than his would: fun *and* savings. Alexandra feels pleased that Her husband respected Her authority and appreciated Her thoughtful gift.

*Genevieve and David*

Genevieve and David met after college in the late 60's. They immediately adopted a Female Dominant Household because it seemed natural to who they were. Recently they have retired and agreed to sell their house and downsize, moving to Arizona to be closer to their daughter's family. The downsizing has required disposing of many items from their life. David finds it very difficult to let go of so many memories, but defers to Genevieve whose authority on whether something stays or goes is final.

This actually makes the ordeal easier on David because he trusts Genevieve's leadership and decision making. He truly believes if She says they don't need something, then they don't need it. She likes the responsibility of the task because David listens to Her, respects Her and does the heavy lifting of getting rid of the items.

She trusts him to do it 'Her way': recycling everything and wasting nothing. Genevieve is also conscious of his emotional needs enough that the ratty old blanket they sat on at Woodstock stays, even though it hasn't been out of the box in twenty years.

*Alissa and Cody*

Alissa and Cody started dating in college and continued for 4 years after graduating before almost breaking up because of the constant fighting. In order to save the relationship, Cody agreed to try and submit to Alissa's natural authority and live in a female dominant household. It worked so well that within a year they were married and living in a house that Cody restored, under Alissa's guidance.

Friday is usually a night that Alissa and Cody have sex but when Alissa returns home from work, She is upset and grouchy from a bad day at work. He asks what he can do. Alissa replies that She loves his full body massages, but just a massage. She's not in the mood for anything else.

Cody puts his leader's needs first and takes pleasure from giving Her pleasure. He helps undress Her and lays Her in the bed. It pleases Cody just to touch his Wife's lovely body and to hear Her sounds of pleasure. He takes great pride in mastering 'Her way' of massage, rather than doing it the way he would prefer, were it him.

Most of all he is happy he can turn Her day around and please Her. Alissa feels this, and knows that Her husband respects Her authority even when She is most vulnerable. Because of this connection the two have formed, She feels Her stress leaving and Her desire returning. She stops the massage and tells Cody to strip naked and join Her under the covers.

That's three different couples from three different age brackets, all working in harmony under a female dominated household. While they are all different, they share some common threads: Trust, putting the other first and accepting fully that She has authority and the final say. Her superior decision making ability is earned but reinforced by the loving support of Her husband. She's the boss.

**Tip!** The easiest way to get a female dominant household up and running is to agree Her decisions are **final** on important matters. She's the boss.

# What It Is Not

What *Female Leadership* isn't, is nagging, bullying and screaming. It's not a means to get your way. For women, it's not a pass to hector and snipe until your sweetheart breaks down and relents. It's not a way to push more work onto your husband and then complain when he didn't do it the way you expected but never requested explicitly. And it's not a way to disregard his feelings on matters that involve him.

For men it is not an abdication of responsibility, carte blanche to be passive-aggressive or a way to avoid making a decision. *Female Leadership* is embracing Her natural strength and planning and supporting it from within. As the leader the Wife may ask Her husband his opinion less but She will also value it more.

After all, if the leader needs an opinion, it must be a serious issue! When the Wife asks Her husband what would he like to watch on tv, the answer isn't 'I dunno, what do you want to watch?'. It's also not 'Whatever pleases you, my Queen.' Try 'I thought we might watch this new show.' instead and accept it if She wants to watch or do something else.

Abdicating authority to your Wife is not an opportunity to both not have to make a hard decision and critique it when it doesn't go to plan. Abdicating final authority doesn't mean you no longer have to make decisions. You still do, but you trust your Wife to choose which decision is the right one and then you support Her fully when it goes well and doubly when it does not. You trust in Her authority and work actively to see Her reign succeed.

## A Few Failing Examples

*Nicole and Tim*

Nicole and Tim have recently gotten a bonus at work. This last year in their marriage has been a tough one. Tim thinks it would be nice for the two of them to take a vacation together. He thinks he could really reconnect with Her and make Her happy. He wants it to be about Her, so She can pick the place and arrange it. Nicole resents that Tim has half-assed this, making Her pick the place and put the whole thing together. She also thinks it's too much money.

Tim offers to do more but he is not good at getting the seats in the plane She wants or using the transportation services She likes. She tells him that She will handle it and the trip will be four days instead of seven. Tim argues but Nicole gets very angry and says Her decision is final. She warns him not to challenge that or he will sleep on the couch tonight. Tim relents because he just wants the fight to end and for Nicole to be happy. In the end it was good the trip was only 4 days because they both spent it resenting each other and doing separate things.

*Karen and Martin*

Karen and Martin have been married for twenty years. Karen has always been opinionated and strong-willed. It was one of the things that attracted Martin to Her. When they were first together Karen led the way in their relationship both in the bedroom and in the household.

Both liked this arrangement. But as time went on, Martin took a more passive role, deferring to Karen on all things and always saying things like 'Whatever you like?' and 'Sure, I guess.' when asked for input.

Over time Karen grew resentful of always making the choices and would be critical of Martin's lack of commitment to helping Her. Martin in turn became passive-aggressive and rather than supporting Her decisions, would subconsciously undermine them and make sarcastic remarks about the failures, making Karen feel overwhelmed with responsibility and worst of all, unsupported and alone.


*Anja and Steve*

Anja is a very direct person and Steve likes that. Anja knows what She wants, especially when it comes to the bedroom. She gives him good direction and he eagerly submits to Her commands. However, Steve believes that Anja is out of his league and he lives in perpetual fear that if he angers Her or displeases Her enough She will leave him. So he kowtows to Her needs and never disagrees or voices an opinion She may not like, even when Anja asks him for his input. Subsequently, though they both seem contented, Anja does not respect Steve at all and he does not give Her everything She needs as a result.

What did those all have in common? Lack of trust, lack of clearly defined roles, lack of understanding. It led to anger, the wrong forms of female dominance and passive-aggressive behavior.

## Why We Need Female Leadership

Did you know a scientific study showed that men who were exposed to female domination videos for the first time had a HIGHER opinion of women after viewing it? Even a week later they viewed women more positively than before and were judged to have LESS aggressive sexual tendencies when viewing porn again, as well as scoring less in tests designed to score objectification of women. Compare that with non-female dominated porn which tends to have the opposite effect on men, increasing the aggressive tendencies and dehumanizing women[1].

---

[1] http://www.dailymail.co.uk/health/article-4220014/50-shades-HEALTH-surprising-benefits-kinky-sex.html

Think about that. Seeing a woman take sexual control of a man causes men to be more docile, more receptive to seeing women as equals or even their betters and has a long lasting effect. Could it be men are hardwired to desire submission to powerful women? Maybe, but the truth of it remains, female domination and Female Leadership has the capacity to help men make better choices.

It is also well established that men benefit greatly from structured relationships with easy, direct ground rules. A great cause of frustration for many men in relationships is not being able to 'figure out' what is wrong, or what She really wants. Women, by nature are not intentionally vague or vapid. However, years of societal pressures telling them they are to be seen, not heard, 'no one likes a nag' and especially the idea that men are individuals and women are more interested in the needs of the group has created a situation where women know what they want, but suppress it or let it bubble up in little furtive bits, leaving the husband ill at ease and constantly guessing if he completed the errands correctly or even picked the right movie on Netflix.

A female led household doesn't suffer from that problem. A Female Leader says what is on Her mind, let's Her husband know what movie She really wants to watch and tells him when he has done something incorrectly, or more to the point, not 'Her way'. Rather than being resentful, the husband is freed from guesswork and emotional reasoning, never his strong suit, and instead tasked with goals and clear directions, something right in his wheelhouse.

Most importantly, Female Leadership is needed for the health and happiness of the woman in charge. So much has been thrust on women's shoulders from birth. They are told to be submissive but also to work harder than a man to keep the household up. They are told to be a whore in the bedroom and a virgin in the house. They are told that the only thing more dangerous than their sexual desires is their strong voice. Those who speak up are labelled bitches and harpies and those who don't are labelled hausfraus and mice. Those in between have their ideas stolen and mansplained back to them.

A Female Leader is freed of this burden, at least within Her own home. Not only is She freed but actively supported and praised by the single most important male figure in Her life: Her husband.

But I don't have to tell you why it's needed. You're reading this book. You don't just need female Leadership for your relationship, you *want* it.

---

**Tip!** - Being direct and explaining what you want done and *how to do it* frees your husband from guesswork and emotional reasoning, never his strong suit, and instead tasks him with goals and clear directions, something right in his wheelhouse.

---

# What is 'Normal'?

Let's talk a bit about normal. Normal as defined, simple means 'usual, typical or expected behavior'. According to an article from CNN, up to 36% of Americans engage in BDSM and 'alternative' lifestyles. Sounds pretty 'normal' to me.

People tend to use the term normal differently. They use it as a way to call out things they don't understand and/or labels and control things that scare them. They call relationships that threaten their ideas of male-female dynamics 'abnormal behavior'.

It's a ridiculous idea and one that conflates the mean with the median. The mean of adult relationships may be the 'traditional male-female' household. But adult relationships do not fall on your traditional bell curve. There are spikes and valleys. There are lesbians, gays, polyamorous relationships, bisexuals, asexuals, male dominated and female dominated relationships, just to name a few. Relationships can and often are a combination of different things. So there really isn't a good median.

What does this all mean? Your desire to have a Female dominated household is *normal*. Neither of you should feel ashamed to have these desires, nor should you be overly concerned that it reflects some larger issue or makes you too weird for mainstream society. Mainstream society is just the name for the public face of every relationship. Not to harp on sex as an example, but the #1 sex toy in

America has and probably always will be the vibrator. An electric tool designed to induce a female orgasm through intense mechanical stimulation. Think about that. That's the baseline for normal in America's bedroom (as it should be, I'm merely noting that it's a machine). The number 2 sex toy? A strap-on. So don't worry about your desires. They're exactly what they should be.

One more thing, while I'm on the subject of normal. You are about to engage in a serious and uplifting discussion about your wants and desires, concerns, fears, hopes and dreams with the person you care the most about. That's wonderful communication, and extremely healthy behavior. That's not just normal, it's something to be proud of.

# SURRENDER

"I couldn't accept that a jarhead like me would want to be led by a woman. I just wasn't raised that way or programmed that way. Programmed was the word, though. Because what I actually wanted and what I thought I wanted, it was like **two different people**. It was Her ultimatum on our relationship that made me try it. It was the first time Her word was final and it surprised me how quickly I accepted it. I just had to surrender to the idea that She was born to lead me and I was born to follow."

-Raul, Age 37

Making the decision for *Female Leadership* and letting go of toxic societal demands on his masculinity and Her femininity.

## Surrender

What does this mean, Surrender? Surrender what, and to whom? In a nutshell in order to serve your dominant Wife in a female led household, to enjoy the benefits of it you must surrender to Female Leadership. The *who* is easy. The husband is surrendering to the Wife.

He isn't capitulating in a war, he is not falling on his sword. He is surrendering to an idea of *Female Leadership*. Inherent in this is the idea of giving up or surrendering the rights to his own leadership. Often this has only been there because of societal moulding of males and females leaving a power structure neither side really wants or is suited to.

Note, this is only his perceived leadership over Her. He is still a leader at work, and he is certainly still a leader over any children in the house. His authority is crucial there, especially as it reinforces Hers. No one likes to be the bad guy, and as a parent you have to share that role equally. Her power isn't supposed to be a lightning rod for resentment.

He is giving up a long and fruitless internal battle that has pitted what he wants in his heart against what has been told to him by years of assumptions and pressures of an outmoded, sexist and patriarchal society. The husband has to surrender himself over to a new idea and way of life. It won't come easy at first because there is literally all of masculine societal programming to contend with, but the first act, the act of surrender to the idea will help begin the journey.

Let's just look at the baggage being given up and the balances being gained in the relationship for both parties:

- Surrendering pre-conceived notions of masculinity.

- Surrendering the insidious and implanted idea that maleness equals authority.
- Surrendering your authority and ceding to Hers .
- Surrendering the ultimate decision making in matters serious and mundane.
- Accepting Her judgment over his.
- Accepting 'Her way' of doing things.
- Putting the needs of the whole ahead of your needs (most of the time).

What it doesn't mean:

- Slavery
- Loss of identity
- Loss of 'me' time.
- Being a guest in your own home.

## What His Surrender Means for Her

You're gaining a lot. You're first and foremost gaining the respect, admiration and loyalty of your closest confidante and biggest supporter. You're also gaining a lot of responsibility.

This is a big move and it's tempting for you too to fall into old habits. You can conflate surrender with weakness. You can take the power without any of the responsibility, but those would do a great disservice to what you really want: Respect.

Your husband respects you greatly to agree to this. He trusts *your* judgement over his own! He trusts *your* decisions over his own. He believes your leadership will bring the family to a better place than his would. Better emotional place, better financial place, better spiritual place. Do you know how hard it is for a man to trust anybody else to do that? You must be one impressive person to command such respect, trust and devotion.

## What Surrender Means for Him

This is it. You're trusting Her guidance, Her strengths. It's scary to go against a lifetime of programming, but while the head says one thing, listen to what your heart is saying. It's scared but pushing you toward it. There's something natural about it. Trust in it and you'll see trusting Her to lead you will also lead you to your own strengths. You're about to be someone who *gets things done*. You're about to become really confident in your abilities and your ability to deliver. You just have to accept Her leadership and yes, even Her dominance over you.

The key to making Female Dominance work in the real world is total commitment and acceptance to the belief in your Woman's superiority. Note, this is not 'female superiority'. You are free to believe that of course, but it's not a sufficiently personal system to base the dynamic of your future life on.

No, you must believe in YOUR WOMAN'S inherent superiority over you in matters of judgement, decision making and control. It's Her leadership you want and crave! Don't set Her up to be undermined from the start by you. She is the leader of your household. Submit fully to Her superiority and then ceding control to Her will be easy and rewarding.

---

**Tip!** If you want to truly surrender you must believe in YOUR WOMAN'S inherent superiority over you in matters of judgement, decision making and control. Its Her leadership you want and crave!

---

## Natural Authority

You will hear this term a lot in the book. You'll frequently hear me refer to 'Natural authority' and its variants 'Natural leadership' and 'Natural Dominance'. There's a good reason for it. This is the very crux of Female leadership. So, if it's so important, what is it?

Natural Authority is the inherent ability to lead, combined with an inborn grace that lends an aura of leadership. Some men have this, like General Patton, but most don't. Your Wife, however, is positively imbued with it. Leadership pumps through Her veins and radiates from Her like a light. A majority of women have this wonderful natural trait, and a majority of women have it suppressed.

Right now, you may be asking yourself if women are imbued with Natural Authority, why don't they run the world? There are many reasons. Some are obvious, some are not:

- Men may not make the best leaders by default, but the simple sad truth is we excel at violence. We are designed partially for violence (It does serve a good purpose as well as a bad one) and have historically used it at every turn. Our genetic capability to fight and hunt lions as well as defend our families from other competitors also means we are quite good at wrestling control of a household through intimidation and outright violence. Even the most pathetic man can destroy almost everything in his sight. He certainly has the impulse and drive to do so. Women are a favorite target of weak violent men. Female leaders are especially prone to this as their inherent qualities and superior man-management cast his own inferiorities in the light.

- Programming. We've covered this before but to sum up, women are told at birth by media that they are destined to be submissive. They are told that the ideal is finding a man and raising children and that he will provide for Her. Their leadership qualities are cast as unnatural, irrelevant and deviant.

- Leaders make sacrifices for the betterment of the group. True leaders have the group in mind. They are capable of making large sacrifices, especially if it will greatly increase the chances of the group. Considering how much of a wage disparity exists even today, it should come as no surprise that many Female Leaders throughout history have taken on a different role for the betterment of the group.

- Some women just don't want to be leaders. This isn't the same as doubting your abilities, this is flat out not wanting the responsibility.

An important aspect to the phrase 'Natural Authority' is the 'natural' part. We use that word for twofold reasons: One it reinforces the idea that this is something inborn. Something not even worth resisting. The woman's authority over the household is natural and just. Words have meaning. We constantly reinforce submissive behavior by constructing and using a language of submission. It is *natural* for the woman to lead. Our brains extrapolate. We are creative mental explorers.

We are helping the man extrapolate from Her natural dominance that his desire to submit and serve Her must also be natural. The whole first step is predicated on the man accepting his surrender as inevitable and desirable and embracing his newfound role as submissive to his

Female Leader and Her natural authority.

Second, and most importantly, we use the language because it's true. All humanity (save for MacBeth) is born of a woman. A woman's natural leadership comes from Her natural strength and abilities. Without women, there are no men. With their XY chromosomes men are half women, not the other way around.

Women are arbiters and creators of life. A child can survive without a man but without a woman it will die. That is an awesome power and responsibility and if women weren't inherently resourceful and strong humanity would have died out a long time ago. It's well established that women's pain threshold is much higher than a man's. Their capacity to survive on less during the lean times is also well documented.

In short, genetics and evolution have created woman to be a natural leader. This gives them an air of authority, one that is confirmed in them by their ability by themselves to withstand incredible levels of pain and then sustain the life of another human being.

---

**Remember!** Natural Authority is the inherent ability to lead, combined with an inborn grace that lends an aura of leadership. Your Wife/S.O. is imbued with this trait.

> **Tip!** Because it is natural for a woman to want to exercise Her authority, it is also natural for a man to want to submit to Her.

## Giving Over to Her Leadership and Control

Congratulations! You two are very lucky to have found each other in a world filled with misunderstandings and middling contentment. You may be feeling out the edges of this thing called Female Leadership and it's probably very exciting and very titillating. That's good. It should be.

But it's also very serious. It's important for this to work that both sides see each other and empathize with the other's risks, rewards and hardships if you are going to share in each other's successes and joys. So let's take a moment to look at what's at stake and what you both are feeling.

### Understanding Her Desire To Lead You

She wants what is best for you both. She happens to believe the best way to achieve that is to guide you and run the household using Her natural authority and inherent leadership. This may be hard for Her to express because Her desires have been suppressed by society and even by people close to Her that see the very qualities that make Her so special as threatening. She values you and trusts you to support Her decisions and free Her to become the best leader She can be, and to be *your* leader. It's a two-way street. As strong and commanding as She is, She cannot do this alone.

*Understanding His Desire To Serve You*

He sees the beauty in your strength. Even if you kept it hidden, it shone through. It intimidated him but enthralls him as well. He is willing to turn his back on societal male programming for you, not just because he loves you but because deep down he trusts you to lead him. He believes in your natural authority and wants to see you succeed in leading the household, in life pursuits and ultimately him. He values and respects you enough that in a little bit he is going to surrender a lot to you.

# Making it official

Okay, it's time to get started on this new life. Take the time to sit down and talk about Her vision. Time to not only lay out boundaries and express roles and desires, it's time to lay out the bold new view for the household under Her rule. This is the chance for the Female leader to lay out what She hopes to accomplish short term and long term, what She hopes will improve in the relationship and what She values the most in his submission.

After that you're going to need to write out an agreement, a contract if you will. Or if you want to get fancy, his formal terms of surrender. Each one will be a little different but they should all contain a few things.

The Submissive's Side

- A promise to respect Her authority.

- A promise to accept Her word as the final word. "I Ken Jones accept that the word of my Wife Hiroki in 100% final in all matters. I promise to support Her decisions and serve the common goal of seeing them succeed."

- A commitment to lift Her up and support Her decisions. To be Her advocate and Her support unit.

- A complete list of matters you formally cede to Her. For instance, 'I Roger Anderson hereby relinquish rights of control to my leader, Averie Anderson, including but not limited to money, budget, vacations, large purchases, chore duty, household matters big and small.'

- A commitment to do things 'Her Way'. (For more information on this, read the section entitled 'Her Way').

- Whatever else you two have discussed and agreed you should do or improve for the sake of harmony.

The Female Leader's Side

- It's imperative that you have an agreement to respect your submissive. You must respect him after he gives control of a large portion of his life to you as much as you did before he did. You must make an agreement to respect his choice to submit to your control and accept your decision making as final.

- A promise to not abuse your power.

- A promise to retain and respect his voice.

This contract (along with the pledge) will serve as the first bridge and your biggest support tool as you make the transition to Female Leadership. After six months or so, once the household is established and you have accepted your roles, it would be wise to review it and adjust/add as you see fit.

## Sample Contract

This is a good base for a contract. For the purposes of laying out examples, it covers many bases. Don't feel bad if your contract is smaller, or for that matter more exhaustive. There are no wrong answers here. Each Female led household is unique. You can make it as formal or informal as you want, as long as it lists out in clear detail and with little ambiguity what the goals are and where the lines are drawn.

---

Contract Terms
Dec 17, 2016

Purpose:
_____ and Her partner
_____ have agreed to alter their relationship and household to a Female Led partnership. Both partners have discussed the matter thoroughly and come into the arrangement willingly. Note:
This new arrangement is to start immediately upon signing of the contract.
Any partner may terminate this contract at any time.

I, _____, agree to submit to the natural authority of _____ and agree to serve Her. I do this willingly and eagerly. I promise to respect Her authority and I submit to the following for the duration of the contract:
Her word is final. I promise to accept Her decisions and work to see them succeed, even if I disagree with them.
I promise to support Her in all matters, to listen, to offer advice when asked and be Her greatest advocate.
I promise to maintain the household, to clean it, make

---

repairs and look after the general upkeep. This includes laundry and yard work.

I promise to do my tasks in the manner that She desires.

I cede control of my finances, including my paycheck to Her and accept Her allowance.

I agree to be in charge of paying the bills from an account She controls for the express purpose of bill payment.

We have mutually agreed that Her authority does not extend to my workplace.

I, _____, agree to lead _____ and run the household. I agree to take on the responsibility of being the sole decision maker and director for the house.

I promise to always respect _____ and his decision to submit to me.

I promise to be mindful of my power and not abuse it.

I promise to retain and respect his voice.

In order for us to accomplish our goals we agree to meet every Friday night to go over plans for the upcoming week. I will lead the meeting and set the agenda. It will end with a recital of the pledge.

Signed _____
_____

Okay, enough already! Let's get down to brass tacks and start the household under Her authority! Time to start reaping the benefits of the female controlled household. You've written up the contract, agreed to the terms, laid out your vision for leadership. What's left to do?

**It's time for him to surrender.**

## The Pledge

The next section delves into the husband's natural submission to his Wife's desires and control. But submission cannot begin until there's been a surrender. Without it you have resistance, passive or otherwise.

A man who thinks this is fun and games cannot be counted on to support his Wife or accept Her dominion over him. At best he will half-ass it. At worst he will sabotage it. That's where reciting a pledge comes in. Does him saying these words magically bind him? No. But words do have power and repeating them has been shown to increase the chances of success, and their belief in the oath.

A pledge is the chance for a submissive husband to affirm his loyalty and submission to his Wife and an opportunity for Her to reaffirm Her confidence in Her leadership. It bonds and underlines the idea of surrender to the idea of Her leadership. It's an easy tool to keep She and he connected and on the same page, as well as an amazing tool for building trust and respect.

Are you ready to begin? If so, I want the husband to turn to the Wife. He can kneel if he feels it would add to the moment, or not. The important thing is that he says the words to his Wife and new leader. If he laughs at first, that's fine. Finish it and repeat it until the words come out with a straight face and eye contact is maintained the whole time. This may take a few attempts. In fact it should.

It's very important throughout this whole process that there is communication and trust. If the husband is laughing or not making eye contact, he's not vulnerable and if he isn't vulnerable, it's not a real surrender. Without a real surrender, a Wife cannot trust She is really in charge. And we know for this to work at all, **She's the boss.** So, wives, have your husband repeat it to you until you are satisfied. Let it be your first command to him as his new leader. And know this: from this moment on, you're in charge.

## The Pledge

"I surrender authority to you.
I am doing this for the betterment of us.
I accept that this is what I truly want, to serve you and to begin the process of lifting you up
and have you as Leader of our household.
I promise to honor you and respect you.
Please accept my pledge, as I accept you as leader
and natural authority of the household."

It should feel different now. The jokes and nervousness and 'are we really going to do this?' should be replaced with a feeling of realness and excitement. The husband serves the Wife now. It should feel like a first step in a real and exciting journey.

## Pledge Examples

*Flannery and Colin*

Flannery is and always has been a very effective Female Leader. However this made it very difficult for Her to date or have long-term relationships in the traditional sense. Oftentimes the confident men She was attracted to would not take to being a subordinate. Add to this that Her culture's predominant belief is that willful women are good, but ultimately they should submit to their husband's desires.

All of this led Her to be very self-conscious and guarded when it came to love and intimacy. Luckily, She moved to New York City and met and fell in love with Colin. Colin is a very confident man, so confident that he happily accepted that his true desire was to be Flannery's subordinate and serve Her many talents.  Flannery is his ideal woman in every sense of the word.

Their five years together have been very successful and gone a long way to reassuring Flannery both as a leader but also as someone who is terrified to be vulnerable. Integral in this is how important the pledge is to Her. Flannery and Colin have a very strict and strident dominant/submissive relationship that many would consider somewhat extreme. Therefore it is important to Flannery that Colin reiterate the pledge at the end of each and every Command and Conquer meeting that they have.

It delights Colin to do so because the words have meaning and it gives him great pleasure to see how his pledge of loyalty to Her eases Her insecurities and makes Her an even stronger and more effective leader of their household and of him.

At the end of the meeting Colin kneels before Flannery and repeats the following, doing so until his leader is satisfied.

"I belong to you. With all my love I submit to you. With all my passion I serve you. With all my desire I obey you. Your word is final, I will never challenge your natural authority. I give you whatever you desire because you utterly possess my heart and soul. I respect you, I honor you, I am devoted to you because I was put on this earth to serve you just as you were put on this earth to lead me. I exist to submit to you. Please command me."

*Hayley and Chad*

Hayley and Chad both agree that She has always been the stronger willed of the two, both in personality and in action. She has gone on to get a high-powered finance degree and now works a very long job that pays very well. Chad is a high school teacher and happy about it. Hayley's salary allows him to not only not work crazy teacHer hours but also take 3 months off every year. Because of this financial imbalance, the two of them agreed that it would be better if She led the household.

However they didn't want to go very much farther than that. So Chad accepted his role as a subordinate to Hayley, but really only to the tasks and the general well-being and household upkeep so that Hayley Herself can do the high-pressure high-stress job that brings them so much joy and travel. So the pledge between them is simple and serves more as a reminder of their contract. They say it only at the end of the command and conquer meeting, which they only have once every 2 weeks.

"Hayley, I accept you as my natural authority. I thank you for your leadership and hard work. I promise to support you in word and deed. I will keep our household as you want it so that you may succeed at your career for the betterment of us. I agree to keep the household your way, as well as accept your word as final on all household matters. Thank you for all you do to give us a wonderful life."

Notice that these pledges all share some common traits:

- An explicit act of surrender, of submitting to the Female Leader. These words must be said. The husband never stops surrendering to the Wife. It is an act of love and devotion to do so. That is why the pledge is not just the start of this adventure but a constant companion.

- Referring to the woman as a 'natural leader' or having 'natural authority'. This is because Her leadership and authority is natural and just. You're not having to create a new ecosystem, but accept the one you are genetically programmed to function the best in.

- Words of praise and thanks. Leader can seem a thankless job. It's important for Her to hear how much you are grateful for Her leadership.

- Honor, Respect, Devotion, Love. These are ultimately the reasons a man serves his woman and why She leads him.

Men, in the first week, but especially the second you may find it difficult or hard to make it work, so when you feel the old feelings coming back just repeat to yourself "I surrender to my Wife's authority. She is my natural leader." Practice saying it out loud. It should feel pretty exciting, and maybe even a little silly at first, but after two weeks it will be who you are. It's proven science that it takes about two weeks to form a new habit. At the end of two weeks you will have a new habit, the habit of a contented man who proudly serves his contented woman.

---

**Remember!** The husband never stops surrendering to the Wife. It is an act of love and devotion to do so and the act reinforces the Leader/follower bond.

---

Women, I want you to take that pledge and personalize it. You may not find that you need to. It fits the bill pretty well, but if you do, go right ahead, I won't take offense. You're the boss!

I want you to use it occasionally in the first month or so. You may find impromptu discussions about what you two spring up quite frequently in the beginning. This is totally normal. What you are both seeking from it is reassurance. What better form of reassurance after discussion than to hear the pledge. From his lips to your ears, his pledge of loyalty will excite and invigorate you. And from his end it will do the same, plus drive home for him emotionally that he is really doing this, and he is really emotionally invested in serving your needs.

So I'd like you two to start crafting a pledge. Write it down on a piece of paper. This first one was a good start and it was important to say it out loud because this journey needs to be taken seriously. But you will need your own valedictions. As you go on reading this book take time to add, subtract and change things from your very own pledge. It should be very personal and mean something substantial to the both of you. But for now, start with a basic outline and go from there.

Secondly, you will have a 'Command and Conquer' meeting every week or so. We will discuss the details of that meeting later on, but I want you to end it with his recital of the pledge. It will feel formal and official and really cement the strategies you have just discussed in the meeting.

Time to make a natural born leader! Time to bolster Her confidence and strength with a loyal and effective subject. Let's begin the act of submission.

> **Tip!** When you have moments of doubt, practice saying "I surrender to my Wife's authority. She is my natural leader." The words will reinforce positive supporting behavior.

> **Remember!** Make him repeat the pledge until he can say

the whole thing seriously, calmly and maintaining eye contact.

# SUBMIT

"I resisted my Wife's authority and my own desire to be led. I drank, I swore, I was unhappy and it just kept getting worse. I was sure She was the best thing in my life and I was equally sure She would leave me. I crumbled emotionally and physically.
From rock bottom I looked up and saw Her reaching out to me. She was so naturally strong and kind. I knew then that She had *always* been above me. I surrendered to Her and gave Her my complete trust right then and there. I found my true happiness when I stopped struggling to be Her equal and submitted to Her natural authority."

- *Anonymous*

"The act of surrendering to my Wife's natural authority was of course fun and exciting. But I was shocked by how much I learned about my Wife when I learned to just *listen* to Her."

- *Anonymous*

## Submission

I have one mantra: 'Submissives are not slaves'. People who don't understand the world of Dominant/Submissive relationships have this mindset that views submissives as wishy-washy weaklings, passive-aggressive and eager for the lash. Often, they view submissives through the lens of pornography or badly executed teleplays that tend to cast submissives as pathetic people (often times with some past emotional baggage) begging to be told they're stupid and otherwise humiliated. While there can be a lot of that kind of play in the bedroom (where it is just that, 'play'), it gets the aspects of being the submissive in a relationship all wrong!

Submissives are actually brave, strong and selfless people. It takes real inner strength to give up some authority and trust in your partner to guide the relationship. Submissives see the whole of the group as worth more to them than their individual demands. And though they give up authority they do not give up agency. I cannot stress this enough, submissives are entitled to their opinions and a good Female leader not only listens to them, She values them. It's only Her decision that is final, but She needs and wants the input.

> **Remember -** Submissives are not slaves! They are timber frames. They support the house.

## So, What Is Submission?

Merriam's describes it as 'The state of being obedient. The act of accepting the authority or control of someone else.' Google has it as 'The action or fact of accepting or yielding to a superior force or to the will or authority of another person.' Boiled down, it's 'The action of accepting the authority of another person.' Now that's very similar to Merriam's.

Let's look at that definition again:

'The action of **accepting** the **authority** of another person.'

I've bolded **accepting** and **authority** here, because these are the two keywords in submission. Nowhere does it mention being owned, or giving up your desires or being a slave. Slaves, by definition couldn't be submissives because they never 'accepted' their immoral enslavement. A submissive makes a very positive and proactive choice to be subservient to another's authority. They **accept** the inherent authority of their Female Leader.

Obviously, **authority** is the other key ingredient in submission. A submissive must strive to accept that their leader's judgement is the best judgement. That She will take advice from the submissive when asked, filter it with Her own knowledge and then come up with the best solution for the household. When She does, Her **authority** must be **accepted.**

You've heard the phrase many times in this book already but it needs to be driven home: **She's the Boss**. When you surrender to your desires and to the idea of serving the group dynamic that is a couple, you accept Her authority, so that She can bring out the best in you and in turn, your support brings out the best in Her, creating a dynamic that bonds leader and worker, general and soldier, Mistress and loyal husband.

---

**Remember -** A submissive **accepts** the inherent authority of their Female Leader.

# From Surrender to Submission

The pledge has been made. The husband has accepted his Wife's natural authority over him and Her leadership of the household. Now how does surrender turn into submission?

Through behavior modification.

By changing your thinking and your doing to a more submissive, proactive support mode you slowly align yourself as a supporter and submit to Her natural authority and Her leadership. It is not until submission is established that we can move onto the ultimate goal and final phase: servitude.

Just as to submit to a Wife's authority a man must surrender, A man must submit in order to serve. Submission is so much more that being submissive in the common sense. In fact, that common sense submission, the physical submission, isn't a necessary or oftentimes useful part of a Female Led household. That's more often a sex thing.

No, real submission and the kind of submission required to make a Female led housebound work is accepting truths about the submissive and the Female Leader, about their new dynamic and what it entails, and accepting things have to be gone about in a different way. This is crucial. There is a different dynamic in play now. The husband has said his pledge, possibly many times, and the Wife is now the boss.

That's a great start but alone it's not enough to sustain a Female led household. Minds have to change and long held methods have to give way to new ways of thinking and doing. I'm going to give some tools and steps that will make submission easier, and in turn make Her leadership flow.

Let's start preparing the groundwork for the husband to serve his Wife.

## The Art of Listening

We all tend to think we are good listeners. Some of us actually are, but even the best listeners could take some hints and tips. Women, even if you have a husband you consider a good listener, I bet there have been times his listening has turned from being a ear to bend to something else. There is no doubt in your mind he heard your words, but he focuses on the wrong details, or offers direct advice about how to 'handle' the situation. I call this **proactive listening,** and it's an extremely common trait across men. To understand what is going on here, you need to understand a bit of how men operate.

Men are by and large doers over thinkers. That is not to say they don't think much, but that we see things as cause and effect. We often learn the most by doing and failing (IE: How not to make a light bulb to paraphrase a famous

Thomas Edison quote) than by listening to instruction. We focus our vision and critical thinking skills on problem solving. It's how we are wired. Evolutionarily it worked to our advantage to be that direct.

When you come down to it, men aren't that necessary to the survival of the species, at least not in the numbers we are in. One man can impregnate many women. Our use is in our ability to improvise and act on the fly, to prove that this young, lone, scrawny outsider is of practical value. We can defend against a tiger in one instance and fashion a splint out of sticks and vines in another. This makes us useful.

But do you see the issue with this? To be effective men must have a problem to solve or a task to complete. We are great at getting things done. But when the Wife is talking about an issue with co-workers, She sees a chance to just sort of vent, let someone hear it, empathize and then get Her emotions back on an even keel. A man hears a problem with inter-office relationships that must be solved.

**The trick to this is understanding that most times, listening *is* the solution.**

But even that is only a half-measure. Men and women listen differently. Men hear details and focus on nouns whereas women hear generalizations and tend to focus more on the verbs and adverbs. Of course this is a massive generalization, but it's still worth looking into. Let's take this story as an example:

"Mary sent Bill to the store to get twelve apples to make a pie. She wanted Granny Smiths. Bill returned with a dozen Galas. Bill liked Galas so he got those instead. Mary was mad and explained that Galas don't work well in pies. She sent him back. Bill returned with six Granny Smiths so Mary would make a pie with a mix."

Questions men would excel well on if there was a listening test would be things like 'How many Gala Apples did Bill get?' and 'How many times did Bill go to the store?'. If you asked them what the story was about they'd likely say 'Making a pie.' and fail to see that this was a story about conflict. Most Women would pick up on that immediately.

So here's the art of listening: for men, listen to Her tell you the story and focus not on the facts around it but the general mood and whole of the story. Pay deep attention to your Wife, read Her expressions as a clue to the mood. Think about how the verbs and actions within the story interconnect to be something larger and less about the minutiae. You'll find She is more satisfied with your listening and you might find you have a deeper understanding of your Wife.

Men should focus more than just their ears when listening to their leader. Eyes should be on Her. It goes without saying that electronic devices should be off or out of sight. She's the center of attention. Your body should be open and receptive: no folded arms, no closed off shoulders and body pointed away. Listening is really an art that encompasses so many senses. Women tend to pick up on nonverbal cues better than men so it is paramount not to accidentally block yourself off or otherwise ruin all the good listening.

---

**Remember!** Listen to Her tell you the story and focus less on the facts and more on the general mood and whole of the story. Pay deep attention to your Wife, read Her expressions as a clue to the mood.

---

## Her Word is Final

We've said this before and will say it again, but **Her word is final**. Just as there is no such thing as free speech if you don't support speech that you disagree with, there is no such thing as Female Leadership if Her word isn't final the second She makes a decision you disagree with. Then it's only play acting.

For the Female Leader there is no leadership if there is no belief Her words will be obeyed. It's not a war and no one lives or dies over this, but at the same time, you've both agreed this isn't a democracy either. It's more like a benevolent dictatorship. Day to day actions are your own, but when it comes to big decisions, the Leader calls the shots.

For the Female Leader, how *natural* will your natural authority feel if you cannot trust that your executive decisions will be trusted and supported? What bad habits might you slide back into without that trust? There are many options but none good.

On one end your authority is undermined and you simply give up on the concept, going back to the way the household was before the pledge - more equal footing perhaps, but more dysfunction, made worse by the failure and ultimate exposure of a lack of trust. On the other, an attempt to use the position of power to reinforce obedience and acceptance of your final word. Let's call this a less-than-benevolent dictatorship. That's one that can easily fall into all-out war between you two, or worse, abuse.

It's crucial this be ironed out early between you two. For the Wife, there is a fine line to walk, but hey, that's the price of responsibility and authority. The fine line is not insisting on final words for simple day to day tasks or activities that have little bearing on you. It should really be reserved for big decisions. And it should come after you have asked for the opinions and input of your chief-of-staff.

By limiting the times where your final word is invoked, you give it gravitas and importance. And by involving the opinions of your most vocal and powerful ally you increase the desire to accept your word (and ultimately your judgement) when you have to make an unpopular decision. After all, this is precisely the kind of decision you are expected to make and the kind of leadership that fueled his desire to submit to your authority in the first place.

For the husband, I have but one question: How can you submit yourself to Her if you ultimately go against Her decisions? Are you serious about serving? Because if you're not, this is the time to say so. Actually it was earlier, but now might be the last time. You wanted this. It only counts when it's a decision you disagree with. It's easy to accept Her word as final when it's what you want too. Remember, She is the leader. It's Her natural authority. A submissive follows their leader.

Trust me when I say life will be easier and everything will work smoother when you accept Her word is final. Your input is not discredited in this situation. As a matter of fact, it's more valued. Nor does this mean you 'need permission' to do your own thing. You're not a child. But when it comes to big decisions (think when and where to vacation, taking a new job, selling the house, buying a car) that's Her bailiwick.

You wanted Her to take on that awesome responsibility, remember? You believed She was better at it than you. Well, time to show it and accept Her authority.

But it's not just that, Her authority must be accepted as the right and natural thing. Accepting Her final word because you both want to make Her leadership work is not a valid reason and it will be undercut whether the man intends to or not. Her natural authority is the true reason you accept it. It must be accepted by both husband and Wife that She has the final say on all things (agreed upon in the contract) because it is the way both husband and Wife were designed. This is the natural order of things. Tell yourself that. There's no questioning what is natural because there is no need to question nature. The sun comes up in the morning. Rain is wet. Leaves fall in autumn. Your Wife leads you. Her word is final.

> **Tip!** Remind yourself that Her word is final because She has **natural authority** and you value Her **superior judgement**.

## Her Judgement is Best

Part and parcel with Her word being final is the concept that **Her judgement is best**. Note, this does not mean the man has bad judgement. After all, it must be pretty good to choose this life and land the heart of such a wonderful leader. It just means Her judgement is better. In that sense Her judgement is best for the direction of the household.

Leaders prove their leadership through judgement and action. On one hand they make tough decisions (Her word is final), on the other hand they know when to make them or not (Her judgement is best). Women naturally have superior judgement to men when it comes to long term thinking and understanding nuance.

Studies have shown time and again men are prone to rush to judgement and seeing things as being a yes or no proposition. This no doubt served men well in the Serengeti or in the vast steppes of the Russian plain, but it's not ideal in a household, either for the day to day minutiae that make up family relationships or when dealing with a creditor, the person writing up your mortgage or the customer service rep at Bed, Bath & Beyond.

There are times when it is appropriate and useful, of course, but those times are still best judged by Her, and then when She gives the command to unleash the power of male monochrome thinking and aggression, it's the right time. By accepting Her judgement is best, when the time comes to act, the man will have the confidence of knowing She wants that action.

Again, it's important that both She and he accept Her judgement as being natural. Biology has imbued Her with some inborn traits, great judgement is one of them. It's an offshoot of Her natural authority. Accepting Her authority and Her word being final as being Her natural inalienable right makes accepting Her judgement as best easy.

## Accept Her Guidance

It's funny that wisdom and guidance seem to be such male-dominated enterprises. The history of philosophy, with a few notable exceptions, is a veritable sausage fest. From Aristotle down through to modern day philosophers and solipsists, philosophical thought is littered with men trying desperately to remove sexual desire from the equation, rationalize it or make it the centerpiece of their thoughts. They tangle with the thorny idea of God and God's role and generally try to come up with the grand answer. It's a useful exercise (literally as brain exercise) but often, the amount of actual guidance that comes from philosophy is next to none.

Contrast this with teaching. This is a female-dominated profession. One of the few, up there with counseling and psychology. In all three of those professions women outnumber men by at least 2 to 1. As opposed to philosophy, these careers are predicated on giving practical guidance.

You can best judge a society by what they find palatable for their children and for adults by when the chips are down. If society didn't think women were better suited to guide them deep down, then they wouldn't prefer them to counsel them when they suffered from addiction, or felt lost and alone.

If they didn't honestly believe women were inherently more empathetic, wise and in tune to social dynamics then they wouldn't prefer to see female psychologists when trying to save their marriage or recover from depression. And if society didn't believe in their core women were more apt to both have and impart knowledge, men would dominate the teaching professions, but the simple truth is they don't.

Even in high school, where rates are the closest to equal, when you take out gym coaches, the numbers line back up with middle schools at that solid 2 to 1 ratio. Not to discount men's contributions to raising and educating children, but let's be honest, the numbers tell a tale.

What does this mean for the Female Led household? It means the man may have to un-train some ways of thinking. Self-reliance is an amazing and wonderful trait but I've yet to meet a man who didn't take it too far.

Men are trained to believe they are on an island, and emotional island and it is up to them to proverbially fashion coconuts into radios. We are taught from early on that emotion is weakness and tears are 'for girls'. I'm not trying to turn every man who reads this into someone who weeps at every sunset, but honestly, women don't do that either.

Can we get rid of this awful stereotype? Your ability, as a man, to cry when a child dies in a movie does not for one second mean you wouldn't put yourself between your child and a pack of wild dogs. So that detergent commercial with the son washing the clothes for his dad and all his Vietnam vet buddies makes you misty every time? So what? Your Wife has seen you take down a tree with a chainsaw like a boss. It was fifty feet tall and it fell just where you planned it.

Guess what, it is okay to ask for guidance from the Mistress of the house. She has wonderful wisdom to impart if you are willing to listen, and more to the point, brave enough to ask. Her knowledge and empathy are two characteristics that allow Her to guide the husband and yes, teach him.

We never stop learning. It's strange that we have no problem taking knowledge from a stranger but cannot take the most valued guidance from our closest advisors. She knows what a man you are. Admitting fears and concerns won't take away your ability to take down a gazelle or build a shelter. It will just include Her in your thoughts and worries. And you will find, She has answers and can take on that burden.

The husband must accept (there's a lot of accepting here, but there's a lot to deprogram!) that his Wife has knowledge and wisdom that can really help him. He must accept that Her guidance is for his betterment and that She has his best interests at heart. It's one of the benefits he should get from his submission.

Her dominion over him is for not only the greater good of the household but his greater good. She has the tools (guidance), the ability (her superior judgement) and the power (her word is final) to help him conquer things that have bothered him for ages. A simple example would be the constant yo-yo of dieting, or drinking too much.

Ava and Henry have been married for 22 years. Last summer their son moved out of the house and went off to college leaving them alone in the household. Ava read about the Female Led household and broached the subject with Henry. He needed no convincing.

Henry has always been a faithful husband and a good partner but his management skills and control issues always left a lot to be desired. After six months however, under Ava's exceptional leadership, Henry shifted his duties from management to support, where he excelled. However, he still had fifty extra pounds he'd had since their son was born. It has always bothered him. He reached out at the end of their command and conquer meeting and asked for Ava's guidance.

Ava understood that Henry tended to snack out of boredom. She offered to help but only if he was serious about losing the weight. Henry insisted he was ready. Ava tasked him with creating a grocery list that She would have final word over.

With the first few lists She scratched off items like pretzels, chips and fruit drinks, replacing them with apples and other fruits. After a few times Henry began making better choices on his own. Ava also told Henry that every time he wanted to have a snack that wasn't fruit, he needed to ask Her permission.

This was not done to be a permanent change or to micromanage, rather to make Henry consciously think about the fact he was snacking. When Henry asked, if he hadn't done more exercise than usual, She would say no. Henry accepted it because Ava's natural authority made it easy for him to accept Her word as final. In three months Henry had lost forty pounds and formed new habits that ensured he wouldn't gain it back, all thanks to the guidance of the Female Leader of the house.

---

**Remember!** Her guidance is there for you and She has much to teach you. But you must be willing to listen and brave enough to ask.

---

## Support Her Decisions

It's not enough to just agree that She has your best interests at heart. It's not enough to just accept Her natural authority. It's certainly not enough to just accept Her word as final. You have to turn that acceptance into support. And you support Her decisions with actions.

Accepting these ideas like Natural Authority is almost a philosophy. Well, philosophy is mostly just thought. It rarely translates into action. Maybe Nietzsche. Actions matter, because they prove the mettle of the man.

If you really believe in your female leader you will show it. We know that 'stepping up' is a thing we should do in a relationship, whether we accept a Female leader or not. We should show up and do our part, but this is something different, something *more*. Your leader will make decisions you don't support on the face, and your disagreement is not necessarily wrong.

There are lots of ways to skin a cat as the old (and gross) saying goes. Men, you are entitled to disagree. Many subordinates have disagreed throughout history. A good leader needs dissenting voices. However, once that voice has been expressed if She has stuck by Her decision, **Her word is final.**

Now is your chance to shine. If you can help Her decision succeed, even when you are on record as disagreeing with it, you will serve both Her and the household. People make mistakes, so too will your Female leader. So too will you.

Your most important job is to support her, humanity and all. If She knows you have Her back even when you don't agree, even when it might fail (despite your efforts to make it succeed) She will truly feel free to make the tough decisions. And let's be honest, you believe in Her ability to make those decisions over your own. Help Her make them with confidence.


*Kathleen and Lowell*


Kathleen and Lowell have been together for a little over a year. Kathleen made it very clear when they were dating that She is the boss. Lowell was reluctant at first but found

Her control over him calming and liberating. Last month Kathleen and Lowell decided that they wanted to build a wall of bookshelves for their large album collection in the basement.

Lowell wanted to get wooden ones that were a little bit pricey and install them in. This meant he would have to mount them and paint them. Kathleen wanted to get the ones from Ikea.

Lowell explained to Her that the MDF would likely sag in the middle, making them unappealing to look at. He also explained he felt confident in his ability to paint them in a reasonable timeframe. Kathleen disagreed. Lowell advised Her again to consider his option. Kathleen insisted on the Ikea ones. They were substantially less money.

Lowell accepted Her word as final. He went and purchased them and installed them for Kathleen. He knew the MDF was going to sag under the weight of the albums so he showed Kathleen that in action with one cubicle. He then showed Her a solution he built: a thin metal slat that is invisible when records are in the cubicles. Kathleen was delighted and told him to go ahead and install them in all the bookshelf cubbies.

When he was done, they had their bookshelf wall and it looked great. Kathleen was very pleased with Lowell and felt very supported by him. She acknowledged that his idea would have been better but with the money they saved they could get more records if they wanted to.

## Trust Her to Lead

There's that word again, *lead.* How is this different from trusting in Her decisions, Her word and Her judgement? Well, it's not and it is. It's all of those things, combined into an action. That's the leadership.

Her judgement, word and decisions are combined to provide a direction for the household, a vision of Her leadership. She has an idea of where She wants to take the family and you. She needs your trust to be up for it, to hold onto Her hand like the man on the cover and follow in Her footsteps.

A special note on spiritual leadership: If the household is a religious one it is worth considering a separate discussion around the aspect of spiritual leadership. Religion is your own very personal belief. It is up to you both to determine who is the spiritual leader in the household.

If it is important to both of you (or even just one of you, and it doesn't matter who), it MUST be addressed at the very beginning. This has the potential to create an imbalance in the relationship if it isn't acknowledged and agreed to in the beginning.

*Julianna and Jackson*

Julianna and Jackson met online on a website that caters to alternative lifestyles, so they entered into dating knowing they both wanted a female led household. They have always dreamed of leaving New Hampshire for Miami, Florida but never had the money or type of jobs that would give them that chance. Julianna has tasked Jackson with running the finances and saving money. Through scrimping, saving and couponing, he has saved 5,000 dollars over two years. He wants to vacation to Miami, to experience it.

Julianna believes that they can move there if they are daring. They do not have children or own a home. Julianna knows that Jackson is an amazing people person who would excel in hotel management. Julianna knows She would excel in hotel planning and labor. She decides that Jackson and She will take night school to get associate degrees in concierge management and Spanish. This uses up almost all of the 5,000 dollars.

Jackson knows Julianna's word is final on this so he accepts it. He also knows it is his duty to faithfully support Her decisions. But even more than that he trusts Her judgement and Her ability to lead them. He is excited in the opportunity and not only excels at his after hours study and classes, but works to bolster Julianna when the work gets taxing.

At the end of their 2 years, they have the degrees and speak serviceable Spanish. Both easily get jobs at the same hotel in North Beach and leave for their new adventure in Miami.

## Respect Her

You may have noticed by now that all references to the new leader of the household are capitalized. It's *Wife, Female Leader, She* and *Her*. That is what is known as an honorific. Just as the title of a great leader like President is always capitalized, so too I honor the Female leader of the household. She is worthy of respect.

Is this kind of deference required? No. But it costs nothing to do it. Little actions of respect build to big actions. They keep you centered and focused on serving. Respect isn't weakness, and no one is asking you to bow and scrape your way out of the room like some slave in a harem. Respect is strength recognizing strength. She has a difficult job and She is mastering it. That's worthy of respect.


## Be the Best Follower and Believe in Her

Do you believe in Her? Do you really? Then be the best follower you can and tell Her that. There will be times when you disagree on something big, and Her word will be final. It's enough to accept Her word as final and commit to supporting Her decision, but it's also an opportunity to shine. Tell Her that though you disagree, you believe in Her ability to lead, and you trust that the decision will work out. Belief from you breeds confidence in Her. A confident leader is a successful one.

Be proactive with your belief. If you find She is not being direct with you, or falling back into old habits, ask to talk about it. Tell Her you see Her falling back into old habits and ask Her what you can do to help with that. That's what you do when you believe in Her leadership and you don't want to see it fail.

## Manage Your Expectations

What are your expectations of a Female Led household? Are you doing it for the sex? Do you expect Her to pick up all the slack? These are important questions to ask yourself. You need to look to manage your expectations.

Yes, the sex should be better, as it would in any relationship that became more healthy and connected. Yes, She will pick up the slack in the leadership department, but you shouldn't have expectations that will only disappoint you if they fail to be met. The goal is servitude. The goal is supporting Her leadership for the betterment of the household.

Now, I'm going to introduce another key point here, one that I will come back to repeatedly. It's a core point, just like 'her word is final' and 'she's the boss'. Like those ideas it will reinforce other ideas as the come along like timber frames in a house.

**Giving in order to receive in return is not submission.**

You will see immediately in the section below ('Change How You Think') how giving with the expectation of something in return is not only not submissive, it's passively dominant behavior. It's a tit-for-tat that you control. After all, if you don't get what you want, the implication is next time you may not give.

Ask yourself, what is the thing you expect out of this? If your primary thought is anything but a better household for you and your Wife through Her leadership, then you need to stop and rethink your priorities. Your expectations are out of whack.

It's not wrong to want a better sex life, more money, and a happier partner out of this. It's wrong to expect those things, and worse to have them as the reason for doing it. She is the reason for doing it. It's okay to desire the other things and even better to hope for them, just don't set yourself and Her up for failure by expecting things that aren't necessarily part of the deal.

## Change How You Think

No one wants you to change who you are fundamentally, and the goal of changing how you think is not to make you into a sycophantic yes man (see 'Maintain your Manliness' a couple of points later), so dispense your fears over the idea of changing how you think. You will still be you, just better. Changing how you think really comprises two key concepts:

- Be less reactive.
- Think of *we* not *me.*

On the first point, people can be proactive or reactive. What that means is people either plan for eventualities and prepare or prevent them from occurring (proactive), or respond after the fact to something (reactive). Nobody is always one or the other.

You will never be proactive on everything, nor should you be, but you can be less *reactive.* Men tend to already be more proactive than reactive because we are by and large, raised in societies that reward anticipatory thinking in men. But we are often terribly reactive in relationships. Hey, why rock the boat, right? The problem is reactive and passive go hand in hand.

It's okay to be proactive if you think something is wrong. The trick is (and part of the second point "Think *we,* not *me*") it's self-centered and poor form to automatically assume it has to do with you. That's just being pre-emptively reactive, if you will.

Proactive behavior takes into account the environment and the knowledge you have learned being an attentive support system for your Leader. If your Wife or girlfriend is more guarded than usual, or closed off, there is probably a reason. A reactive person *reacts* to this guardedness by say 'Hey, what's wrong?".

They aren't asking that entirely out of altruism. They're bothered by the attitude and change in routine. And yes, they also want to help, but the way is wrong. It will only make someone more guarded.

The proactive person takes into account the environment and what they have learned. Then they set the table for talking about it, or not if it doesn't need it. Maybe that co-worker has been bothering Her the past few days, safe bet that might be the cause. A proactive partner knows this and takes away some of the worries around home but doing a little extra, then later asks how work is going. If that was the case, the proactive partner listens and offers emotional support and advice if asked.

Now for the second point: men are raised to think of themselves first. Evolutionarily this made sense for millennia, but it really doesn't now and it certainly doesn't in a female led household. Even though She is your leader, I promise you She thinks of *we* over *me.* This is one of those natural, inborn things that make women such excellent leaders. Thinking of *we* over *me* does not negate the self, in fact it adds to it. Humans are always stronger when they don't go it alone.

A nice example of thinking *we* over *me* is giving for the sake of giving. As I mentioned in the section 'Manage Your Expectations', giving in order to receive isn't just not submissive thinking, it's egotistical. Think about it. You're only giving in order to get what *you* want. There's no submission in that. Heck, there's no acknowledgement of the other person in that. It's a barter system, something every six-year-old knows.

Giving with no expectation of reciprocation, on the other hand, is true submission. It should make the giver feel as good as the receiver. Maybe not at right first, but a change in thinking will lead to a rewarding sense of being a part of something greater than yourself. You may find yourself actually feeling like you *serve* something greater than just your base desires, because you do. You serve your Wife.

One place that this sees a real positive benefit is in the bedroom. There is a lot of stress put on women to perform, even on dominant women. Male sexual success is often based on achieving an end result. It's a very quantifiable yes/no proposition for men, if you think about it. For most women it isn't.

Sexual pleasure can include the orgasm but doesn't have to. Thinking of sex as a two act play that ends with an orgasm encourages a laser-like focus on achieving that orgasm. As a man, I can tell you this really isn't our fault. Biologically, that's our goal. If we are being honest, biologically the female orgasm is near irrelevant to reproduction. But we are also great thinkers and not ruled by our baser desires, so we have the ability to *change our thinking*.

Sex shouldn't be about the end result. In that sense, giving for the sake of giving in the bedroom removes those pressures and feelings, it removes racing to a finish and more accurately resets expectations. I think you'll find that it resets desires as well.

A submissive husband might find great sexual and emotional enjoyment in giving in the bedroom with no pressure to deliver a conclusion. The simple act of touching, for instance, is a wonderfully sexy and intoxicating act, one that does not often get its due, instead relegated to a checkbox on a list of foreplay one *has* to do before moving on to the the main event.

> **Remember!** Giving in order to receive isn't just not submissive thinking, it's egotistical. Change your thinking and you'll find joy in giving.

*Practice tips*

Right, so it's one thing to say we will change how we think, it's another to put that into action. How does one do it? Through observation and modification. Here are a few tips to help.

For Her

- **Call him out on it.** Gently, of course. This isn't him being a jerk, it's him having to recondition after years of societies bad and influential training. If you suspect he's being extra good to 'earn' something like time out with the boys, tell him you appreciate the extra effort but ask him what it is he really wants. You're the leader of the household, not Mommy.

- **Acknowledge the effort.** So it's not 100% altruism on his part. He still wants and deserves positive feedback when he is being that 'giver'. Your smile, your purr of happiness, your words of encouragement and satisfaction are a gift that is worth so much to him. His submission isn't just about agreeing to the superiority of your leadership, it's about pleasing you. Let him know when he's done it! I cannot stress enough how this one thing (positive feedback) has the power to lead to making him a giver who truly thinks of *we* over *me.*

For Him

- **Review Your Thoughts.** You do this already, likely. It's just that the part of you that wants to do it to get the reward wins out. This doesn't make you a sociopath, it doesn't make you greedy. It makes you normal. But you're not normal, you're special. Review them again and see why you're really cleaning the cat box or giving that neck rub. If the answer is it's an ends to a means, find that right time to talk about what it is you want. You have rights and you can go out or watch the game. You're not a slave, and She is not your parent.

- **Don't second guess your instinct.** Don't get in a battle with two sides of your mind. Your first thought is almost always the correct one. So, if your first thought was 'this will get me the new tool I wanted', you know you're not being submissive. If your first thought was "She looks like She needs some help with the shopping.' don't second guess that good thought!

- **Think 'what do I expect in return'?** This is similar to 'Review your thoughts' but more direct. Sometimes it's obvious. We devise plans to get what we want. But sometimes our motivations are hidden, even to ourselves. If you don't know, be direct and ask yourself that question. If the answer is Her happiness, great. If it's a chance to go out with the boys, take a moment to think about what that means. Because that's a great example of passive undermining of authority. It's passive because the actions are done in the dark, even to yourself. You may not know it but you are using your submission as a bargaining chip. Secretly what's underwritten when you use submission to get your desires is a very non-submissive threat to withdraw your service if you do not get what you want.

*Vanessa and Richard*

Vanessa and Richard have been married for eleven years, the last five of which have been under Her leadership. Richard is a model submissive supporter in every way but one: in the bedroom. He is not a selfish lover by any means, but he still tends to lead the narrative, even when Vanessa is 'in charge'.

This isn't his fault, he's been raised to think of sex having the goal of completion. The sense that sex is a reward for his submission and one that has the ultimate goal of both his and Her orgasms has removed a lot of adventure, has led to him passively dictating the flow of their lovemaking and has led to Vanessa's sense of sexual satisfaction dwindling.

After reading this section of the book together Vanessa uses the 'command and conquer' meeting to address these issues. Without criticizing Richard, She explains that a lot of what was described is how She felt. Richard apologizes and after thinking about it comes to realize he has been passively leading it with one goal in mind. He asks what he can do. Together, he and Vanessa discuss some strategies.

The next time they are intimate, Richard asks permission to follow is game plan, with the important caveat that She stop it whenever She likes. He leads Her to the bedroom, undresses Her slowly and gently and places Her in the bed. Richard then spends the next half hour just exploring Vanessa's body, touching, squeezing, teasing. He takes time to enjoy areas he never paid much attention to and takes cues from Vanessa as to what She likes and does not. He does not focus on his needs or having an expected conclusion.

After a certain period of time, Vanessa instructs him on using his hands to please her. Because She is not expected to have an orgasm, it actually comes relatively easily. Richard feels an enormous sense of satisfaction knowing he truly thought of Vanessa's needs first and only and was able to make Her feel satisfied.

## Maintain your Manliness

Remember the time you saved that stray dog or the time when the hurricane hit and you had everything prepared? You cooked a meal over the fireplace and made sure there was enough water to drink and gas for the generator? Because She does and She loves those memories. She loves when you're a man and can reach the highest thing on the shelf. She loves when the leaves have to get done and you just get them done. Period. Men are fantastic at a term I call **getting things done.**

What this means is we really shine in a crisis. Most modern crises do not compare to the ones of old. But they still happen and they still cause stress. When the move date is fast approaching and it's going to take 24 hours straight of packing and lugging boxes, men excel at this.

The task may be herculean, but it's also simple: *move the boxes.* This does not seem overwhelming. It is a simple problem with a simple solution, just get it done.

Your Wife sees this value in you. And Ladies, if you don't see it, know that it is there and cultivate it! Reward him with Hard work geared around simple tasks. Give him the day to take the leaves. Tell him where you want the pile and let him attack it with a methodical yet astounding pace.

She doesn't want you to sacrifice one iota of what makes you a man when you submit to Her authority. It's that part of you, plus many others that makes you such a good support for her. You're *Her* man. So vacuum and do the dishes if that's where you're most helpful, but still be brave, chop wood and take charge in emergencies when that's what is called for.

If submitting to your Woman hurts your machismo, just breathe and remember that's normal. You've been trained to believe that serving a woman makes you *less* of a man, when in fact your ability to recognize Her qualities and ability to let Her direct you towards your own strengths and qualities is actually the opposite.

There is nothing more than confidence that isn't boastful arrogance. Retrain that wounded pride into something else: pride in your craft and productivity. You're amazing!

### Lynn and Orin

Lynn and Orin met 25 years ago while still at college. Lynn got a business degree while Orin got a degree in animal husbandry. Orin wanted to work on a farm like his parents had, and he desperately wanted Lynn to be his wife. Lynn had bigger ideas and believed in Orin's ability to work a large farm.

In return for accepting his marriage proposal, Orin agreed to Her word being final, Her financial control over the household and Her natural authority.

Fast forward a few years and Her tight budgeting and decision making allowed them enough money to buy a struggling farm. Lynn trusted Orin to run and manage all aspects of day-to-day life on the farm, to cultivate connections and revive the productivity of the land. Essentially, She valued his manliness and competence to do his work, while still accepting his submission.

Rather than being weakened by this situation, Orin thrived. Orin not only retained all his skills, being free of other obligations actually made him more focused and better at his work. Orin works long days making the farm productive and successful, at night when he returns home, he tends to needs there and goes about the pleasurable and relaxing tasks of serving his wife.

Lynn works to maintain the business side of things, selling the products they make and maintaining the budget and distributor relationships. When the day is done She loves nothing better than to come home to Orin's care and devotion.

## Understand Femininity

Femininity is more than the natural grace and beauty that is woman. It's also a LOT of work. Let's say you like Her 'dolled up'. If you live with Her you know how much work that can entail. The better you understand femininity, the better you can make that part of Her life easier and more enjoyable.

This has benefits for you both. Women, things tend to be softer and more gentle. There's a reason their undergarments and blouses are referred to as 'delicates'. A lot of time and care goes into making this things clean and neat.

You have a great opportunity to understand the art of femininity and show it in your work. There are a million little things She does, some of which She will always have to do (like primping), some of which you can do for her. She can fill you in on a ton you could do for Her but here are a few examples:

- Latching a bra and putting it in the zip sack before running it through the wash.

- Handwashing silks and stockings and hanging them gently.

- Learn to read labels and follow the care instructions exactly.

- Use Fabric softeners.

- When you pass by it, clean up Her vanity area. Make sure it's stocked with wash towels for makeup removal and Q-tips and various other sundries.

When you do these things, it's important that you take the time to learn how She does them. This is Her routine. You won't be helping, no matter how much extra responsibility you take on, if you do it wrong.

## Put Her First

What does this mean, 'Put Her first'? Quite simply it means put Her needs ahead of your own in not just action but thought. Catch yourself when you think things like 'but I want to do this' or 'I want to do this, how do I convince her'. That's putting yourself first.

Don't forget you have needs and desires, you're not a slave. But serve Her needs first. Train yourself to think of

Her needs as a checklist to be run through before you get to your own. Then you'll find it's so much easier and more natural to serve Her. And when you get to your needs, you will enjoy them with a guilt free satisfaction that comes from a hard day's selfless work.

## Be Yourself

No one should be asking you to fundamentally change who you are. You're changing some actions, and modeling some new behaviors, but you are acquiescing to something that is as much inborn in you as in Her. By this point in the book there should be no doubt in your mind that you want to submit to your Wife/partner.

I hope that you have accepted that this is a core part of *who you are.* And since it is, you're not changing who that person is. You're bringing a part of your personality up out of the darkness and into the light, embracing it and accepting it.

This won't fundamentally alter who you are on a daily basis, how you interact with your friends or your sense of manhood (not negatively, anyway). So relax and recognize you are augmenting who you are. These actions and behavioral modifications are all about making a wonderful household for your leader but She doesn't want a fundamentally different personality. You are the one She fell in love with.

Your commitment to this journey, Her leadership and who She is only makes Her love you more. So be yourself. Don't second guess yourself anymore. One benefit of Her leadership is She will be more direct with you and you will know when something isn't right and you'll know it early. So you can free yourself of the head games!

## Sofia and Crawford

Crawford has always been a craftsman. He has always had a bit of difficulty connecting to people and reading them, but when it comes to crafting, he understands detail and nuance. In high school he was already making advanced woodcarvings.

Sofia has always been successful and driven. She was a 4.0 student in high school and college. However, She always had trouble with relationships, until She met Crawford. What other men saw as bossiness and an un-feminine forcefulness, Crawford saw as directness and lack of ambiguity. They fell for each other immediately.

It was Crawford who initially suggested Sofia be the leader of the household. He came across the concept while looking for solutions to the lack of directness in modern relationships. Sofia was intrigued but worried that it might change Crawford. She laid out in their contract that he had the right to refuse actions if he thought they were changing who he was. As it turned out it was unnecessary.

Sofia's leadership and directness allowed Crawford to be who he was. His natural desire to please Her was brought to the foreground under Sofia's leadership. Her directness freed Crawford from second guessing himself or trying to 'read' Sofia. His positive responses to Her forceful nature put Her at ease and allowed Her to be comfortable in Her own skin.

Together they bought an old craftsman house and Sofia tasked Crawford with restoring it, including every last wooden crenulation and bit of filigree, which allowed him to be himself while contribution something of great value to the woman he loves, worships and serves.

## Prove Her Right

In every action, deed and thought you have a masterful chance to **prove Her right.** It's tough to be a leader. It's a great responsibility to be the boss, to have the final say on everything. She has to make tough decisions that go counter to your wishes at times. She has to make the tough decisions that affect not only Her but everyone in the household. Being a leader is something not everyone is cut out to be. Your Leader believes She is that person for you both. It's up to you to prove Her right.

You prove Her right:

- When you support Her decisions, even the ones you disagree with.

- With your actions and attention to detail.

- With your happiness.

- In becoming closer to Her.

- In accepting Her natural authority.

- When you support Her through failures.

- When you laud the brave victories.

- When you think of Her first.

# SERVE

"I did not know what joy it would be to have such a powerful, confident man obey me without question. It delights me how much joy he takes from serving me. In just 5 years time I have been promoted 4 times at work, partly because of the hard work my husband does at home but mostly because of the confidence I feel having the complete support, devotion and submission of someone I respect the hell out of and adore."

-Kara, age 29

"I thought I'd like it. I was wrong. I love it. I never listened to my coaches, my teachers or my friends, but I listen to Her. Having Her word be the end-all-be-all has freed me to be myself."

-

Blake, Kara's husband, age 30

# On Her Majesty's Secret Service

It's time. Pledges have been made, he's submitted to the idea of Her natural authority and worked on how we think and interact, he's embraced new roles and your goals. Now you are ready to turn his submission into Her service.

This section is devoted to making his intentions and actions into concrete results for Her leadership. In order to help turn actions into results, this section will provide tools and ideas meant to sculpt the Female led household that She desires. There will be many points you have seen already, just fleshed out and laid out practically in a way that allows you to use them immediately. As usual, the Mistress of the house should feel at liberty to pick and choose what She sees fit from this box of tools.

## Define Her Authority - And His Strengths

These definitions below should be a checklist used to determine how deep Her authority lies. We already know things like Her word is final. These definitions of authority are on a larger scale. By now, some things should have been ironed out or at least discussed.

Generally, couples up to now probably have discussed specific tasks like laundry and car maintenance. But these are subsets of a larger arena of control. It's this arena we need to define now. It's time to define the scope of Her dominion and put it into practice!

So I advise using these definitions as a checkbox. It's not exhaustive, but it should help start. Look at the types of control and what they entail, and then She should say which She wants dominion over and which She doesn't. If She does want something like financial control, both parties should then outline what that entails, written down in detail (to be later added to the contract) to make sure there is no vagueness or misunderstanding.

Be sure to personalize this list with your own. Each type of authority below is an important section of the household, and one that should not be left up to interpretation. When subordinates are left to guess at best it's needlessly stressful for them, at worst it's a recipe for failure.

## Financial Control

This is an extremely common choice. It's also a great one if both parties are up for it. Money is the #1 cause of stress in relationships so being able to remove just this alone would be worth it. Financial control takes many forms, however. It can mean that the purse strings are controlled by the Woman of the house and this could entail everything from physical control of credit and debit cards to allowances, to monitoring every purchase made by Her submissive. But it can also be the opposite.

She can set a rate of expenditure and a target savings goal and delegate paying of bills, budgeting and savings to the submissive, essentially tasking him to deliver. It can also fall in between, for instance saying that he is on a fixed allowance and is given access to one account for the express purpose of handling bill payment.

You can see there's a lot to be determined here. Be sure to spend the appropriate amount of time to iron this one out because if you can, you will find enormous monetary and emotional benefits from it.

## Executive Decisions

Another extremely common one. This one is very straightforward. Thinking of buying a car? Executive decision. What to use the end of year bonus on? Executive decision. These are by and large one-time decisions of a somewhat memorable nature. Where to get take-out is not an executive decision. Deciding to build an extension to the house is.

This one is the one most likely to see a challenge to **Her word is final.** It's why I recommend that declaration being part of both the contract and the pledge. Just like free speech is never a problem until someone says something you disagree with, Her word is final is never a problem until it conflicts.

## Household Dominion

Whose house is it? Obviously it's both, barring some previous financial arrangement. But even in non-Female Led households it's often the Woman's house. So, it's a relatively simple question to answer, does She have household dominion? What does that mean for the arrangement?

Define it. It could mean everything from deciding where frames get put on the walls and furniture gets placed to when and what color you paint the guest room. These are not day-to-day decisions. Think more like maintaining the house long term and its general layout. Some couples are fine with defining this as simply as 'Will take his input into consideration but Her word is final'.


## Day to Day Decisions

These are the decisions like going to the grocery store today instead of tomorrow and making sure the laundry is tackled. It is not what show to watch on TV that night or what take-out to get. That's called micromanagement. But if there are several tasks that need to be done and they take more than a day to do them, She gets to decide priority.

This is often an easy one. Falls under Her house, Her rules. Any man who truly wants to serve his Wife would want to do it in the way She most desires.

## Task Delegation

Though tasks do fall under day-to-day, delegating whose responsibility they are to begin with is something She can have control of. This is another common one. It's common for many reasons, not the least of which is men are very good at accomplishing tasks on a list. More on that later. But it's common because it's easily written with easy to measure deliverables.

Is doing the laundry part of his service? Pretty easy to tell if that is getting done. Is making sure the bathrooms are clean and stocked his job? Another easy one to tell. Many couples like this one in particular because like the money issue it takes up previously thorny issues and ends them. He hated vacuuming and always resisted it but no more. Her word is final and he accepts Her natural authority.

## Controlling the Ways and Means - Not just what to be done but *how* to do it.

This one can so easily be confused with micromanagement, but it isn't that at all. Micromanaging would be standing over someone and critiquing how they are folding laundry or how they wash dishes. That's a nuisance and a bother for both parties. It's also done out of a lack of trust in the abilities of the submissive to do things the way She wants them done.

Controlling the ways and means is different. It's establishing the way things should be done ahead of time, not during. It's doing things **Her Way.** I will go into greater detail about that later because it's a key point to the harmony and success of a Female led household. For now, know that this is an option when establishing and defining Her authority over you. She can control the style in which things are done as well, or She can not.

## Physical Obedience

Physical obedience is a lot of what people who know nothing about a dominant and submissive's relationship think it looks like. This isn't really something for the faint of heart and honestly, if you are interested in this I suspect you are both already in a pretty strict D/S relationship.

This one absolutely must be outlined. If Her expectation is that in this new relationship you will serve Her tea and then kneel obediently next to Her or face corporal punishment, you probably want to know that ahead of time. If this is what you both want, congratulations on finding each other.

## Sexual Control

Subset 1A of physical obedience is sexual control. This is a large category and if it is something that is part of Her authority over you, it really must be defined. Sexual control encompasses a large area.

It can mean She is the instigator and controls when sex will happen, or it can mean She physically controls you during sex, or it can mean She controls your orgasm, keeps your sex organ locked up in a chastity box during the day, or any combo of these. It's pretty important to lay out what it entails, or at least what it doesn't.

*Eliza and Ruben*

Eliza and Ruben have just entered into a long term relationship. Eliza has never hidden who She is from Ruben. In order to become boyfriend and girlfriend they have set out the terms of Her natural authority over him and his service to her. Eliza enjoys power and being in control, but doesn't want to micromanage Ruben or lord over his decisions. So they agree that while they are out on a date Her word is final and She controls the day to day decisions.

When Ruben stays over at Her apartment She has dominion of the household and sexual control over him. However Ruben is free to be his own master whenever they are apart. She has no interest need or desire to control him financially or delegate his tasks.

*Kendra and Gordon*

Kendra and Gordon have been married for 10 years. Early on in their marriage they adopted a Female Led household. It started out simply enough. Kendra's word was final. They both enjoyed the way this cut down on division and stress, so they added to Her authority.

First Gordon was put on a weekly budget, then he was tasked with paying the bills. This removed a lot more stress from the relationship. By year five She controlled Executive decisions and the day-to-day decisions. By year eight Gordon and Kendra had ceded total household dominion to her.

Gordon was provided a list of routine tasks to accomplish and how Kendra wished them to be accomplished. He excelled at the repetitive tasks, growing in confidence in his ability to do things **Her way.** Now at year ten, both are more happy and in love than before and Kendra feels like an effective leader with excellent judgement.

## The Concept of 'Her Way'

There are several ways to accomplish a task like folding laundry. These ways could be the quickest way, the most efficient way, the laziest way, the way that best fits the drawers or even the way that makes the least amount of creases. But there's only one right way, and that's **Her way.** Why is Her way the right way? **She's the Boss.**

Sounds a bit pushy, doesn't it? Even a bit like micromanagement when I phrase it all like that. But there's a darned good reason Her way is the right way and it has nothing to do with Her word being final. The simple answer is you're doing this, *all of this,* to serve her. You want to make Her life easier and less stressful. You don't want to be micromanaged on a task any more than She wants to micromanage you.

There's a reason the army teaches you to peel potatoes the army way and it's not about stripping individuality, it's about your C.O. not having to worry about watching you make dinner, instead entrusting you to do it and do it right every time so he/she can get down to the business of commanding a company of soldiers.

This is where the concept of '**Her way**' comes into play. One of the biggest gripes I have seen in couples, female led or not, is disagreement not over who does what but over the very *way* things are done. People are stubborn. They have their ways for doing things. The ways often don't have any practical differences compared to other ways, but none of that matters.

Constantly debating over how the laundry is folded is annoying, constantly debating over how the laundry is folded, how to vacuum, whether to pay for daycare with a credit card or check, what type of gas to put in the car, how to make the bed and where the heavy pots and pans go in emotionally draining. And when the emotional battery is drained the mind makes mistakes and the body breaks down. This affects you **both.**

This is why Her way saves the day. Men are great doers. We can tear through a good list like no one's business. If that list is annotated, great! If it isn't we will attack the jobs the way we see fit. That doesn't matter when it comes to mowing the lawn or taking out the trash but it's not the best for something more personal, like putting away clothes or washing lingerie. For those details it's often the whole process that needs to be done, not just the end product.

So I have one piece of advice for you men:

Embrace **Her way.**

This is what devotion is really about. Doing the hard work that makes Her leadership shine is a wonderful thing, but being conscientious enough to do it Her way? That's true submission, love and devotion.

Accept Her way and let Her teach you the way She wants it done. Is your way faster? Maybe. More efficient? Possibly. The way She wants it done? Nope. Your goal is to please Her. Your goal is to show She matters by paying attention to the finer details.

Accept that and you can be taught how to do things Her way. Once you are doing them Her way, you'll never have an argument, or feel undermined in your duty (imagine putting away all this laundry you cleaned and folded yourself only to realize She took it out and re-folded it) or resent her.

You will also feel something else: pride. There is something for a submissive when they are exacting and excel in elevating the well being of their mistress. There is a pride in work and craft. There is a wonderful feeling of acceptance and joy that comes from this level of commitment and respect for Her.

Finally, though doing things Her way may take a little longer, it'll be less tiring. The physical battery is your strongest battery. Leaving the emotional alone, and the confidence you will feel from seeing the second-guessing and inspection of your work go away will make the work fly by.

## Teach him **Her (Your) way**

This is where you come in, female leaders of tomorrow. You no doubt have a way you like bras folded and put up, a way you want skirts put away, a drawer for blouses, etc. You have a way you like to do your laundry (two dryer sheets, easy on the detergent), a place you expect to find potholders and baking utensils, a way you manage accounts and file important documents.

You have a vision in your mind of not just what would get done with the support system you desire but *how*. There's nothing wrong with this. Embrace it! Get what you want out of this because you will give him so much in return.

Show him your way. Trust him to learn if after a few tries and never have to worry about it again. This is not micromanaging. This is teaching. He is going to do his best to listen. Teaching is great because it eliminates the need for nagging. A job learned the proper way and executed that way needs no supervision. A lesson taught provides no nagging or badgering. After your way in place you'll never have to come close to micromanagement because things will just run smoothly.

One note of advice. It pays to be explicit. Show him the steps, praise him when he gets it, and be supportive when it takes a few tries. He's stepping up here.

---

**Tip -** It pays to be explicit when showing him your way. Show him the exact steps, praise him when he gets it, and be supportive when it takes a few tries. He's stepping up here.

---

## Getting Things Done

Just as women have a natural authority, men have a natural ability to ***get things done***. Again, evolution as a lot to do with this. Years of walking/running the savannahs followed by hardscrabble endless toil in farms has made us efficient pack mules designed for maximum functionality and singularity of purpose.

Our minds are vessels expertly tuned and timed to sense a stray sound or something out of place and to recognize larger patterns like wheat cycles and weather disturbances. These traits come from a historically harsh world that punished those who did not have these traits.

Our efficiency has led to some interesting differences between the sexes. Women see more variations of color than men. Men track fast-moving objects better than women. Women are capable of withstanding more severe long-term pain caused by illness or disease, whereas men are capable of withstanding more long-term use after injury. All of these things obliquely point to our strengths and weaknesses. And that strength for men is our ability to plod ahead, single-mindedly until something is done.

We have all been there: That instance where the move date caught up with you and you wonder if there are enough hours in the day to get everything from apartment A to apartment B. Men excel in that kind of crisis. Why? Because we have an easy objective that is only rendered hard by the level of effort.

Understanding what needs to be done is not hard: Move your stuff. The task may be herculean, but it's not overwhelming to us. It's a challenge. A challenge that is accomplishable with just enough time and effort. So you start lifting boxes, and you lift boxes until there are no more boxes to be lifted. Then you clean up the old place, hand over the keys, get the deposit check and sleep for 10 hours.

We do not excel at things that require nuance, generally speaking. We can handle and handle well small tasks that require nuance, like writing a thank you note to an aunt and uncle. But writing fifty of them? We'd rather be tasked with writing out the addresses and stamping the envelopes.

Okay, but how does this apply to serving the female leader? By taking all we have learned so far, trusting in that and then **getting things done.** You accept Her word is final, you take on the tasks She lays out for you. You listen and take instruction on how to do things 'Her way'. And once you have that you get to work taking tasks that seem overwhelming to others, but just a matter of time and effort to you, because that's how you're designed.

Freeing the decision making allows for a great leap forward in productivity. Being given exacting measurements and requirements leads to getting it done right the first time and a deep satisfaction in a job well done.

## It's A Team Effort

She may be the leader but it's a team effort. Mistress and willing servant still makes a team and a team works together to combat issues. These topics below apply to you both.

### Lift Her Up With Your Words - Lift Him Up With Your Praise

Be positive! Everybody needs reassurance. Everybody needs validation. Being the two most important people in each other's lives, your words are doubly important to each other. For the man, take the time to tell Her how great a leader She is. When Her decision pays off, acknowledge it. When it doesn't, support her.

Tell Her what you appreciate about Her leadership. Be sure - especially early on - to tell Her what you like about the new arrangement. Let Her know you not only accept your submission to Her, but like it and see the value in it. It's important She knows Her leadership and dominance over you is beneficial for you as well as for the household and Her.

For the Leader, it's important to praise him. He is serving you and his servitude is fed by your approval and happiness. Acknowledge the special things he does to make your day brighter. If he has listened to you and adopted Your way of doing things, make note of that.

Give him praise and validation. This is not just for his own well-being but your own. By acknowledging your submissive and being thankful, it keeps you humble and keeps the possible tyrant within at bay.

## Anticipate Her Needs But Ask Questions!

It's important to develop a rhythm in submission. There are many things that are regular needs, demands and actions. A good subordinate learns to anticipate Her needs. If She likes tea after dinner it's wise to have the water ready to go on the hotplate.

If She takes a bath on the weekends, have everything She needs ready to go in the bathroom. It's comforting and makes your job easier. But this doesn't mean you should be expected to know everything!

Ask questions! Find the right time to do so and use it to get to know Her better. Questions are your friend. She is the leader and as such She has Her way. If you don't know what that is, ask. There are no stupid questions. As you begin this journey it will be uncharted territory for you both. She may not have all the answers, but She will have some, and asking Her is the best way to find it.

For the leader, it's crucial to be patient with the questions, *especially* in the beginning. There's a lot changing, and a lot going on. What is obvious to you may be completely oblique to him. Remember, you're good at nuance, he likely isn't. So take the time to answer his questions in a thorough and constructive manner. It's worth it! You're going to get a lot of great service out of him, especially if you empower him with the information he needs.

## Give Honest Opinions - When Asked!

A submissive is not just a worker bee. You don't lose agency over your mind nor do you lose the wealth of knowledge you have gathered over the years. You have opinions and they are varied and valuable. The difference between a submissive husband and one who is not, is the submissive waits until he is asked.

This should come as no surprise. In a world where Her word is final, Her decisions are final and She has the authority, it's expected that the submissive's opinion is asked for, not just given freely. This works for both of you. For one, the submissive is absolved of needing to make a hard decision allowing them to excel at other talents. For the leader, Her word is respected and She is not bombarded with passive-aggressive suggestions that amount to 'I think you are doing it wrong'.

This doesn't mean a submissive husband or boyfriend will not be asked their opinions. A leader values the input and knowledge of Her subordinate. When needed, particularly on hard decisions or decisions where Her knowledge and judgement are not superior to his, his opinion and advice is sage and valued. A good leader doesn't try to partially absolve Herself of responsibility for failure by bringing Her subordinate's opinions in. By asking his opinion She hopes to avoid failure at all.

**Remember -** Just because She asked for your opinion doesn't mean She has to accept it. It's your job to trust in Her superior judgement and support Her decisions with your words and actions, especially when you don't agree with them.

## Combatting Issues Together

Issues need to be combated together. Her authority may lead to the decision, but his actions will support and remedy it. There will be times when responsibility needs to be shared. Take for example if there are children involved. There will be times when the submissive needs to play the bad guy or be seen as the authority. She may have to support his decisions in front of the child, the key is to combat these things together as a unified front.

## Command and Conquer

Nothing proves devotion and submission like listening and then doing. Nothing helps a leader lead like the right forum to delegate, review and tackle new challenges. The **Command and Conquer** meeting is just the thing for the Female Leader and male servant to get on the same page and get to the business of serving Her needs.

The CAC should be held at least weekly. Some couples like to have it more frequently. The meeting should be tailored however She sees fit but it should contain four key elements: Planning, Q&A, Safe Space and the Pledge. They should happen in roughly that order. I'll ay out what each is and why they're so important to the concept of **serving Her needs.**

- **Planning -** first and foremost Her desires and needs are discussed. Remember we *think of Her first.* You are in the business of serving Her now. She's the boss. All concepts you've heard 20 times in this book. Now here they are in practice. Here's where She gets to dictate what exactly She wants while you listen attentively.

- **Q&A -** This is a section that helps flush out the wants and needs into actions. For him, it's a good time to ask what the priorities are around tasks, what serves Her best and how to achieve it. For Her, it's a great chance to show him **Her way.** She should initiate the Q&A by instruction Her submissive it is now an ok time to ask questions.

---

**Remember -** There are no stupid questions. A question means you both have an opportunity to get it right and prevent a problem.

---

- **Safe Space -** This term is getting much maligned these days as some sort of weakling's sandbox, but this isn't a political debate or a college campus. It's a meeting held between two people who love each other, two people engaged in a new, and somewhat scary lifestyle. The safe space is needed and it truly needs to be a judgement free zone. This is his one real time to bring up concerns, fears or even terms for renegotiation of his terms of submission. The beauty of it is it keeps it regulated and helps to remove undue emotion from it. Term renegotiation done in the heat of the moment usually doesn't go so well for either party. But given the time to separate feelings from concerns allows him to present the concerns filtered for emotion, distilling them closer to the actual root of the problem.

- **The Pledge** - No better time than at the end of the meeting for him to recite his pledge of faith and devotion to you. It's a lovely, satisfying exclamation mark to all that has been agreed and discussed, and a lovely reminder for him of who he serves and why.

## Helpful Hints

**What to address in it and what not to -** It's a good idea to limit what is discussed in the meeting. The CAC is great for strategies, big ticket items, small ticket items, tasks, plans for the next few days, odds and ends. It's a great place to talk about things surrounding the Dom/sub relationship and the contract. It's not the best place to discuss family issues or issues outside of the relationship.

It's not the place to talk about your day. It's a meeting, stay focused.

**A space for negotiation and advice -** It is a good place to negotiate terms in the contract, to add to or remove from it, to talk about terms. Because once the meeting is over and the week is on its way, that time has gone. It's not useful or ultimately very helpful to try to negotiate a task in the middle of it, or explain to your leader you no longer want to vacuum the house when it's time to vacuum.

Likewise, it's the perfect place to give advice and guidance to your submissive. While you should feel free to pull him aside at any time to instruct him, bear in mind it's disruptive and can lead to micromanagement, so if it can wait until the meeting, for both your sakes it really should.

**Listening patiently -** There's an art to listening. It's not waiting for your turn to speak, it's not offering unsolicited advice at the conclusion to Her story. It's absorbing Her words, connecting with the feeling She is presenting and asking questions at its conclusion, through that you find what your value and use is to Her needs.

**Planning out the week -** Lay it out, ladies! Make lists! Plan days. We love to have a list to tackle. It plays to a submissive's strengths and minimizes misunderstanding. This, I cannot stress enough, is the opposite of nagging. This is commanding, and we respect that.

**Striking while the iron is hot -** I might recommend doing this around a window of time where you might be free to do other things. You may find as the leader than having your directions listened to so patiently and your authority so validated has made you interested in your husband in other ways. From his perspective, serving, pleasing you and saying the pledge are likely to have done the same. It's not a bad idea to have the option to strike while it's hot. Nothing like deeply connecting intimacy and pleasure to reinforce Her command and his desire to serve!

# Common Problems and failures

If you're expecting this to click right off the bat and run trouble free, you're not being reasonable. There will be problems. There will be conflict. The earlier you can nip these things in the bud the better. As always, the best cure is talk. Talk about what is at the root of the issue. Talk about what you both want. Reinforce together what you both are after. The Wife is in charge and the husband supports Her. Remind each other that you *both* wanted it this way.

## For the Leader of the household - Warning signs

Your man will most times happily serve the needs of the house and you. Sometimes he may do it with a grumble. Hey, we all have bad days. This is normal.  What isn't normal is behavior that persists, or a change in attitude lasting a more than a day or two. here's some behaviors to look out for and how to address them:

- **Failure to continue to do things 'Her Way'.** This is a surprisingly common fault. Its commonness stems from the fact that many things may be causing it. First and foremost, your strong soldier may be overworked and afraid to disappoint you. He values your happiness over everything else, and because men can be so goal-oriented, failure to deliver on even one of those goals can crush their spirits. So in order to keep up, they may cut corners. 'Her Way' is the first thing to go.
  **Solution -** In whatever space you have carved out for your 'command and conquer' talks, look at the workload and ask yourself if it is too much. If it is too much for you, tell him that you have overtasked him. It's not a failure, instead he has heroically worked through an amount of work you yourself couldn't stomach. Create a safe space for his pride while acknowledging the problem.

- **Passive-aggressive behavior -** Your authority is likely to be a bit intimidating. And submitting to you will likely lead to a bit of resentment at times and certainly a period where he figures out how and when to 'stand up' or speak his mind. This is totally normal and expected. The most common

115

way this manifests early on is in passive-aggressive behavior. Cutting comments, sentences with a hint of venom to them, running hot and then cold.

- **Solution -** The key to this is to call it out calmly and directly when it happens. Don't be afraid to say it's passive-aggressive but then follow up with a question of your own. Open the floor to him to express what is really bothering him. It's early yet, you will run into kinks. If he feels validated, and feels you listen and are aware, the passive-aggressive behavior will go away and he will wait to bring issues to the appropriate time in your Command and Conquer meetings.


- **Questioning your authority -** This is another common one. He engages in his work and serves you for the most part but at times chafes at your commands or even worse does not acknowledge your word as final. Maybe he offers unsolicited advice or doesn't support your decisions very well when they go against what he wanted.
- **Solution -** If it happens early on, it's just boundary testing. Be as firm about your boundaries as you see fit. If it happens later on, it's time to renegotiate terms of the contract. It may be he does not want to submit to your authority across all the things you have agreed, or it may be he is acting out due to something else. Either way, the safe space is the place to discuss this.

## For the man - Warning signs of your behavior

- **Internal conversations -** Having a conversation with yourself after your leader has given you a command. This conversation is like a mini-argument where you win. This is okay from time to time, but if it is a common occurrence, it's a problem.     **Solution -** If you feel overloaded or not listened to, when you sit down with your mistress at the command and conquer meeting, ask to have a moment to discuss something, when She sees fit. Don't interrupt the meeting flow or demand it be addressed at the beginning. Your place is support. You will get your turn. If there isn't a problem with your level of work or being heard, take some alone time to repeat your pledge. If you need a shorthand, repeat after me: "I surrender to my Wife's authority. She is my natural leader." repeat it until you feel calm and centered again.

- **Talking back or interrupting -** If you are impatient to get started and don't want to listen, remember who you work for. Pleasing Her **IS** listening to Her. She is taking on a large responsibility planning and having the final say. Respectfully, She needs you to listen. She's giving you exact details so you can accomplish your tasks Her way. And remember, 'Her way' is the only way.

---

**Tip -** If you're having doubts or talking back, remember you agreed at the beginning that 'Her way' is the only way. You value Her knowledge and cherish Her authority.

---

## More serious issues

Now for the thorny issue of when your mistress crosses the line. No one likes to talk about it, but it does happen. There is an imbalance of power and liberties can be taken. I have said it time and time again and will continue to say it throughout this book that submissives are not slaves. What does happen sometimes is that because your mistress has such a position of power Her Authority can tend to go unchecked. Oftentimes this is not a problem as both sides would like it that way, but sometimes it crosses over from commands to abuse.

That is never okay no matter what you may have agreed to. The best way to deal with that is to remind Her that She agreed to respect you as part of this deal. You two will have created a contract at the start of this laying out your hopes and dreams and desires and also setting some ground rules and promises.

You promise to respect honor and serve Her and in return She promises to take care of you but also very importantly respect you. If this is crossed over into abuse verbal, physical or whatever form than She no longer respects you. You have the right to demand that back.

## A few working examples

*Alika and Daniel*

Alika and Daniel are 6 months into their new female dominated household. So far it has been a great success. Daniel has, for the most part, excelled at supporting his Wife in Her new leadership role. The household has improved, and both are happier than they had been before. Alika is extremely proud of Her husband and takes every opportunity to tell him.

However, in the last month or so, Daniel has met expectations and supported his Wife but the work quality has slipped. Alika doesn't feel like Daniel is sabotaging Her or not giving his all, however, the things that are getting done are not getting done 'Her way'. Laundry is not folded the proper way, and the dishes are not being put away fully dry.

Alika takes a moment to review all the tasks Her supportive partner takes on in a week and looking at them, realizes they are far beyond what She Herself could complete, let alone complete to the high standards She holds. At their command and conquer meeting, when it is finished, Alika takes a moment and praises Daniel for his fantastic work. She also explains that She has overworked him. She goes out of Her way to explain that it isn't a matter of his failure, in fact, the failure is Hers: He has been Heroic under unreasonable and **unsustainable** requests.

In doing so, She allows Daniel to take on help without admitting failure. It's crucial to their Dominant/submissive relationship that Daniel understands he is exceptional, and any help comes only because no partner could be expected to sustain those levels. Alika explains that thanks to his great work, their budget has swelled and they can afford a cleaner to come in every two weeks to remove some of the burden. Daniel objects, but Alika's word is final, and because She is confident and supported, She makes that clear and Daniel happily accepts.

*Caroline and Ian*

Caroline and Ian have been partners in a Female dominant household for 5 years. Caroline wanted it more than Ian, but after much discussion, they came to an agreement and Ian took the pledge. For a long time things improved and both reaffirmed to each other the benefits of Her leadership and authority over the household and Ian.

However, for the last six months Her authority over final matters has been routinely challenged by Ian, especially in matters of weekend planning. This has undermined Caroline's authority and made them both less than ideal partners. It could not come at a worse time as they are trying to get pregnant. Caroline worries about this unresolved conflict bleeding into the household, especially when children arrive. Ian worries that his parental skills will be diminished when a child arrives.

When their weekly command and conquer meeting has ended. Caroline requests a frank discussion, separate of standard rules, to talk about the problems they are facing, and their common goals. The talk is acrimonious at first because the problems have been going on so long, the root causes are hidden behind the resentment from petty squabbles.

Caroline eventually defuses this by admitting that as the leader of the house and Ian, She let the underlying issues go undiscussed for too long. Once Ian feels he is being heard and can let go of the minor squabbles, the real discussion begins. Together they recognize his fears about being a father in a female dominated household and agree to rewrite the contract. Ian is given more say in budgetary matters (Though Caroline's say is still final) and a new set of agreements are written in surrounding children and their raising.

Both parties are satisfied and harmony is restored. Caroline asks Ian to repeat their own personal pledge as a sign of his commitment. Ian repeats the words "Caroline, I belong to you. You are the strength and guiding force in our lives and I respect your authority. I trust in you and promise to support your decisions. Your word is final."

Happy with the mutual understanding and respect that they have come to, they opt to strike while the iron is hot and make a baby.


*Samantha and Peter*


Samantha has had a very hard and stressful day at Her law firm. When She gets home Peter has dinner prepared. He seems to be sulking because he ate alone, even though he was warned She would be late often this week because of a big case. At the end of dinner they have their command and conquer meeting. She asks him if he has anything he wishes to bring up. Peter defers.

Samantha asks him to draw a bath for Her. "Yes, your highness." he quips sarcastically. The comment ruminates and ruins an otherwise relaxing bath, disrupting Her at the time She needs Peter's comfort and support the most. At the end of the bath Samantha calls Peter in. She tells him She didn't like his tone and asks him again what is wrong. She tells him She values and respects him and is concerned that he does not seem happy. Peter explains that he was upset She missed the meal he prepared and that he was being petulant. He apologizes.

Samantha reminds him of the contract and pledge. She reminds him of their goals and plans and that he wanted it as much as She did. She asks him to repeat the pledge to Her 3 times. Saying the words in Her presence centers him, and reassures Her.

He is no longer resentful, instead supportive, submissive and sorry. Peter is now eager to make up for it and help his leader relax ahead of Her big case. Considering She is feeling stressed and also a little excited by watching Her loyal husband reaffirm Her importance and value, She takes him up on the offer.

### Gertrude and Martin

Gertrude and Martin have been in a Female Led relationship for a little over a year. Gertrude has always been bossy, but Martin understood this going in. However over the last three months She has taken to not listening to Martin. She also takes out her frustrations on him when she has had a bad day and criticizes him for every little thing.

Her dominance has drifted over into verbal abuse. At the weekly command and conquer meeting Martin explains that he is not a doormat and he demands her respect. At first she does not like this and chastises him again. But Martin remains firm, verbal abuse is not okay. He loves Gertrude and believes in her, otherwise he would leave the relationship which is **always** the right of both parties. Gertrude relents and apologizes. They redefine the terms of the contract, restricting her chances to abuse the power until such time as Martin feels safe.

# Conclusion

There you have it, save for the bonus section ahead. Hopefully this book has reinforced Her desire to listen to Her natural authority and step up to being a leader of men (at least in the household). And hopefully it has emboldened his desire to surrender, submit and serve Her to the best of his abilities.

I wish you both the absolute best in your adventures ahead and confess I am excited for you both as you start this wonderful and life-fulfilling journey together as woman and man, Wife and husband, leader and supporter. There will be trials and tribulations, disagreements, even resentments at times, but above all else there will be immense satisfaction, joy and we'll bring felt by both of you as you move into this novel new arrangement that speaks to both of your strengths and bonds you together in ways most people will never know.

Well, this is it, that's the end of the book. Why not take this time to finish with a pledge? Hopefully by now you've written one that is very personal to you both and affirms his loyalty and eagerness to serve while acknowledging Her natural authority, poise and acumen. Take this moment to close up this book and start your own with an affirmation of what makes you both so unique and special.

# Bonus Section

"The sex was amazing. After a few weeks of being in charge, I felt like I wanted to do it more than I had in a long while, and I felt beautiful, confident and for a lack of a better word, kinda horny."

-Kaylie, 34

## The Naughty Bits - Serving Her in the Bedroom

Well, you've made it to the bonus section! I promised this at the very beginning of the book. There's nothing in here that you haven't seen on the internet probably, but by all means, read through it, enjoy it and maybe discover something fun and new for you both. There's just one thing to remember about the naughty bits...

## It's Her Way Here, Too

Remember, **She's the boss**. If She wants *you* to take charge in the bedroom, that is just as important as respecting Her final decisions in the boardroom. Don't be surprised if She wants you to be the aggressor in the bedroom. Many CEOs revel in a submissive sexual role.

**I want to add a very important caveat here:** No person has the right to force you to do anything you don't want to do, no matter if they are dominant over you or not. Submissives are not slaves and sexual submission is not a blank check to assault or intimidate. Beyond that, if you are game to serve then you serve Her here too.

## Pleasing Her through Attention

Let's focus on the act of pleasing her. It's more than obeying. It's about appreciating. It's about reading the moment right and taking time to create the mood. Taking time to let Her body know you are in tune with it and Her mind know you're focused on the act of loving, not the end product.

That is not to say an orgasm is a bad outcome. It's a great one, and sometimes sex will be definitely geared toward delivering that big O. But it's a bad way to think of sex and sexual pleasure.

For one thing it puts immense pressure on Her to perform. Failure to come could be seen as failure to appreciate all the hard work Her good foot soldier has put into the act of pleasing her. Survey after survey from Masters and Johnson and on down the line have shown pressure to perform as being a major hindrance to achieving female orgasm.

Second of all, it makes intimacy all about sex and it makes sex a race to the finish line. It takes the mind a while to catch up to the body, that's just evolution. Physically our autonomic nervous system and hind brain react almost instantaneously to stimuli. Just think how quickly you can move when startled. Or, if you want a more sexual example, how quickly a nipple can firm up and become erect from just a simple breath of air across its surface.

If you don't slow down the act of lovemaking and take time for both partner's brains to catch up and fully engage, you run the very real risk of the body being finished before the mind has time to get undressed! That release may be physically satisfying or you and your leader, but it's not mentally all that satisfying after the dopamine wears off and it's not terribly intimate.

Here are some styles and acts geared toward slowing it down and engaging Her body and Her mind.

*Sexual Touching*

Sexual touching is the art of exploration without the explicit goal of orgasm. Make no doubt, it's sexual, it's just not expressly for the purpose of climax. The principal behind it is that the whole female body is lovely and worthy of attention.

The back of Her knee is a very sensitive place. Her thigh in your hand feels wonderful. When is the last time you kissed Her just above the ankle or on the top of Her hand? The curve where Her ass meets Her leg merits a little one-fingered caress. You get the idea. Don't set a goal on it. Just explore.


*Devotion*

Devotion is a specific and delightful subset of sexual touching, where the man makes his adoration felt with every act, not just touching. This runs the gamut from foot rubs to bringing Her breakfast in bed to more risqué provocations like...


*Body Worship*

Body worship is one of the ultimate favorites amongst submissive and dominant, partially because it reinforces the status quo for both sides but partially because it gives great enjoyment to both sides. But it's not just for a dom/sub relationship. Any man should take delight at being able to touch every inch of Her and bring forth from Her sounds of enjoyment and pleasure. It's a surefire sign that he is doing a great job.

And what female, leader or not, doesn't want to be lavished upon. Having the very physical connection of your husband loving and taking the time to appreciate you and all of you is extremely reassuring. It lets you know as the Female Leader that your husband worships the ground you walk on and thinks that you are a fantastic leader, a leader worthy of adoration. Nothing beats the sense of touch.

Massage is a great example of body worship for any couple. It's slow, patient, focuses on Her whole body and gives a chance for Her to feel your adoration and you the chance to really appreciate the amazing strong woman before you.

## Oral Worship

This is a specific offshoot of body worship. It is precisely as it sounds. The husband in this case takes extra special care and delight in pleasing his Wife's vagina orally. The woman tends to lead this style of play. She may prefer his gentle exploration of Her with his hands, or She may prefer his tongue and mouth.

Often it's a combination where the husband is allowed to explore and takes his cues off Her sounds and movements. It's different from traditional oral sex in that the act is generally slower and more concerned with taking time to bring about waves of pleasure more intense and long lasting.

There is a subset of Oral worship called facesitting, or queening, where the dominant woman sits directly on the husband's face while he pleases Her orally. Couples that prefer this technique report several benefits including enjoying the power play aspect of it, an increased surface area of pleasure for her, and for him, enjoying Her femininity more intensely and with more of his senses.

Let's put this all together into an example.

*Melinda and Jake*

Jake worships the ground his leader Melinda walks on. He takes extra special delight in making sure She feels like a leader worthy of praise and worship during the week, so She is relaxed and happy when She feels ready to be intimate. It is always Melinda's choice on when and how to be intimate, but every few weeks She will let him know She would like to be worshipped. This is as much for Jake's benefit as Her own, because he craves the hour or so that he gets to simply touch and explore Her divine body.

Jake prepares the guest bedroom for Melinda, by lowering the shades and lights and putting a heating pad into the bed. When he is ready he invites Her in the room to strip and position herself comfortably under the covers. He then puts on soft music and lowers the lights. For the next hour, he lifts up the covers, exposing only the part of Melinda he wants to massage.

By limiting how much of Melinda is exposed he keeps Her comfortable while building up suspense and desire in them both. He works every muscle on Her body from the hands and feet up to the neck and back. When She is

131

relaxed he begins the slow process of working to more intimate parts, gently exposing more of his lovely Mistress.

Since Jake's goal is only Her pleasure and not an end result, Melinda is relaxed and receptive, so as his hands move over Her skin, Her desire builds until She is ready for a release. That is Jake's queue to transition to giving Her oral pleasure. His reward for his devotion and worship is to taste, hear and feel Her powerful orgasm.

## Femdom

Femdom is shorthand for 'Female Domination'. This is a sexual style (more than an act, it is often a host of acts) where the Female is the authority and in control of the ways and means of sex. In porn it often comes with a heavy dose of humiliation and abuse.

There are aspects of it that involve torture. However Female domination does not have to involve torture. It can be anything along a spectrum of ordering the submissive male to rub Her feet to whipping his testicles with a riding crop. The key is Her control of the sexual situation. She may choose to bind Her submissive in ropes or chains, or order him to kneel. Kissing and worship are common.

Female Domination also does not require actual sexual situations to be considered a sex act. Femdom is a legal form of business in many states because the acts involved in it do not technically cross the threshold into sex. Being spanked, tied up and verbally abused, while being highly sexually charged, do not involve sexual touching or orgasm. Having said that, behind the closed doors of your bedroom, it can and will get sexual.

The key to Femdom is mental control of the male submissive. Denial and teasing are common tools of the dominant. This often extends outside of the bedroom. Mental games involving seeing how long the submissive can deny urges, combined with delicious teasing can heighten anticipation and build desire leading up to the time behind the bedroom door. The key with any form of domination is trust and having safe words.

If this is of interest to you both I suggest avoiding porn as your first example and instead reading about female domination in books and stories. www.literotica.com is a great and free resource that offers stories geared towards all types of sexual play, including Femdom. Since these stories are read and vetted by a community of actual persons engaged and interested in the lifestyle, they will give you a much more realistic and healthy understanding of femdom than pornography will.

## MaleDom

Maledom is the male equivalent of Femdom. The same rules apply about safe words and trust. A man who is submissive to his Wife during the normal events of the week may be called upon to be dominant in bed. This can go from being the sexual aggressor to actual physical domination and bondage.

If this is of interest to your mistress, embrace the role but make absolute certainty that you understand what is desired and wanted. Everybody has a dominant side and a submissive side. You can tap into both. Use your own understanding of the submissive desire to color your dominant actions.

I would like to take a moment to talk about a specific subset of Maledom: the rape fantasy. This is a very common fantasy among women. I say that because I want it understood that there is nothing wrongful or shameful about having the fantasy. It's a fantasy. But fantasy and reality are not the same. Fantasies are often impractical.

If you want to practice it out as a loving couple I recommend a few things:

- Read up about it on safe chat groups and sites dedicated to couples exploring D/S. There are a lot out there.

- Establish firm ground rules and safe words. This is for his emotional state as much as hers. He wants you to enjoy it, but he needs to know it's still for fun.

- Start off with only a little bit of the fantasy and build trust from there to expand on it.

- There MUST be a clear signal for stopping play, with no hesitation if needed.

## Strap-on Play

This one is relatively new in the modern consciousness, though historically there is evidence of women wearing makeshift penises dating at least back to the Hellenistic period, perhaps even longer. For those who don't know what strap-on play entails, a woman uses a strap-on dildo to reverse traditional gender roles. She can enjoy the act of receiving a blow-job or anally penetrating Her partner. Dan Savage of *Savage Love* used a contest to coin this sex act 'pegging', a name that has gained acceptance.

This is a particularly novel, relatively safe (there is a learning curve) and very exciting form of sex play. There are several reasons associated with its popularity:

- It's an extreme form of role-reversal. The woman is the sexual aggressor and enters the man. There is a lot of trust and intimacy involved in this act. Some women enjoy the experience of seeing how the other half lives, and more to the point, knowing their partners have too.

- The male prostate is an often underexplored sex organ. For many men it is a unique and extremely pleasurable experience. Some men have reported 'internal orgasms', that is, an orgasm occurring without penile stimulation.

- There are many types of strap-ons, including ones that are 'rooted to the female' via vaginal insertion, connecting Her to the act of penetration and creating a sensation akin to male pleasure, especially in models that combine pressure on the clitoris, vaginal wall and so-called G-Spot with vibratory stimulation.

- For those into dom/sub play, it is a wonderful toy for exploring male submission.

- Finally, it's a unique and bonding form of sexual expression that combines novelty, titillation, vulnerability and deep pleasure. Many couples report feeling more connected after engaging in this type of play.

Some notes: be forewarned, the anal cavity is not a naturally empty place. There is some pregame prep required for this one. Even with that there may be accidents. It's recommended that it be done over a towel for the sake of your sheets.

There are many popular brands of dildos and harnesses. I recommend looking at www.babeland.com (a sex shop with discreet shipping whose products and management are female-focused) to search for your first strap-on. If She is interested in feeling the sensation as well, the *Feeldoe* brand is safe, ergonomically designed and reviewed highly.

A few final notes:

This list is by no means exhaustive. The internet is your best and worst guide. There is a lot of information out there and a lot of rubbish. But there's certainly enough out there to get your mind racing. Don't rush to find every fetish that strikes your fancy. Enjoy the slow roll of discovering what works and what doesn't. Allow what is unique to your relationship empower the desires and thoughts that make sex so rewarding.

# 15 Guidelines

Here is a condensed set of 15 guidelines from this book that you can use as a quick reference. It's a pretty good yardstick to measure commitment by. If you find you are adhering to 12 or more of these (the first 5 being non-negotiable) then you are probably doing a bang-up job of serving your mistress.

1. Surrender to your wife/girlfriend's natural authority.
2. Submit to Her leadership.
3. Serve her.

4. Remember Her word is final.
5. Believe that She was born to lead you.

6. Accept your desire to be submissive.
7. Don't lose your manliness.
8. Change the way you think. Think we instead of me.
9. Put Her needs first.
10. Learn to listen.
11. Accept Her guidance.
12. Accept Her judgement is best.
13. Support Her decisions.
14. Giving in order to receive is not submission.
15. Say the pledge.

# 2017 addendum

## Silent Support

This section exists solely for one person: The husband reading this book that wants this lifestyle but doesn't think his Wife shares his interests. Let me caveat this section before I offer any advice:

1. If this lifestyle is what you truly crave, you need to talk to your Wife about it. You owe it to Her. Chances are She doesn't want it. Only 15% or so of

women are comfortable being the alpha in a relationship. And be honest, your feelings aren't going to go away. She deserves the right of knowing this part of you and accepting (or denying) it. She deserves to know your real feelings.

2. You cannot trick a Wife into being leader of the household. People are leaders, or they aren't. Yes, everybody can lead a group given the right circumstances, but those circumstances come from happenstance, not from Machiavellian, behind the scenes machinations of their significant other. If discovered, there is no way this looks good on you or your relationship, because to try and change someone to meet your desires can only be manipulative and selfish. There is no good that can come from that.

Now, there is a way to become a better spouse to your wife, that will take the built-in desire you have to see your Wife succeed and blossom, without establishing a female led household or manipulating her. There is a way for you to become a more supportive spouse and create a more equal household without trying to trick your Wife into domination. And I mean to give it to you. It's called *Silent Support.*

Silent support is building your Wife up through subtle changes in yourself and your behavior, all with one clear goal in mind: The enrichment of your Wife and Her sense of self. **This is not inherently submissive!** Every true partner should just naturally want to see their companion succeed. There is nothing self-subsuming in the act of praising and acknowledging your partner's successes, nor is there anything self-belittling in lifting your partner up through trust, respect and faith in Her abilities.

The silent part comes from keeping this change internal. There is no need to inform your Wife you intend to be a better spouse. It's almost impossible for that to come off as anything but you wanting brownie points. Silent support is a gradual, un-chaotic change to your behavior, bringing it in line with a more empathetic mindset and outwardly focusing your desires.

When done correctly, your Wife won't notice any incremental change, instead noticing three or four months down the road that She is more satisfied, regards you as more of a true partner and feels more confident in Her life in and outside of the home. It won't be because of some trick you have played on her, or secretly convincing Her that She is a dominant woman.

It will be because you chose to really try to see Her as an equal, recognize all the things She has to do as a woman that you yourself do not (just think about the time difference it takes to get ready in the morning and ask yourself if the shoe were on the other foot, would you spend so much time making yourself beautiful to the world?) and try in earnest to be as good a partner as She is to you.

As Her confidence grows She will become more of a leader in Her own life, without necessarily leading you. But again this is not a secret trick to try and 'con' Her into domination. Alright, with all this in mind, let's look at *Silent Support.*

- **A pledge minus submission -** Give yourself a pledge, one you will say only to yourself. Because this is not a dom/sub relationship, you should remove any submissive aspects from it like 'obeying your Wife'. Promise instead to think of Her first, to respect Her and to try to make Her life easier with your actions. Pledges have a way of reinforcing the behavior cited within.

- **One selfless act every day -** Try and do one selfless act for her every day. Does she do the dishes, maybe find time to do it. Fold towels, pick out the trash from her car. Any little and unexpected thing. Don't call attention to it or yourself. That's not selfless. Over time she will notice and the fact that you did it with no expectations besides her happiness will not go unrewarded. But you're not doing it for that. You're doing it for her.

- **Find a small thing you can do for Her every day -** Does your wife make a cup of tea every morning? If you get up first, have it waiting for her. This is a routine of caring. It's a soothing ritual, meant to connect your actions to Her comfort. It's emotionally reassuring and delightfully intimate.

- **Take on new tasks -** Start with one new thing, like scooping the cat box, and simply take over doing it. Don't announce it, just do it. Keep doing it until it's established routine and established as your job. Then add another. Don't overburden yourself and don't rush it. But over time, you'll ramp up to the duties and cool Her down.

## #Metoo

Since original publication a profound and amazing women's movement has emerged: The #metoo movement. And if you don't know what that is, it's women calling out their sexual harassers and by and large being supported in their decisions. It started out on Twitter (hence the #) but it's spread out into the mainstream and brought down powerful people like Matt Lauer and Harvey Weinstein who abused their power to harass women. Though there have been some notable cases where the harasser was a woman and or the victims were men, by and large it is a woman's movement for women's voices. It's a crucial movement that shows no signs of slowing down.

It's important to understand what makes #metoo so revolutionary. Historically women have not always been their best allies. Women have been taught and trained from a very young age to see *each other* as the real threat to their upward mobility and to use weapons against each other that stay generally outside the view of men. This is due to external forces upon women, not some inherent aspect of female sociology.

And whatever television shows would have you believe about cattiness and pettiness in general and matriarchal societies that kind of thing does not exist. That is more of a product of limited resource and limited opportunity in a male-dominated world.

This is why the me-too movement seems so different because it is a woman lead woman driven movement. Women are by-and-large supporting each other openly and without question and unconditionally. It has the potential to be fundamentally society changing. There are a lot of people (mostly men) who don't want to see that change.

We as men have a great opportunity to help here, but bearing witness, and assisting with support from the sidelines. It's not our place to lead on this one. But we can help foster the movement by being an ally that listens, that acts as an amplifier and *above all else* believes the victim.

It should come as no surprise that a Female Led household fosters that support.

Now more than ever, every female led household that could be healthily and happily enacted should. Not just for the strength and support it provides your Wife in the home, but for a real positive reason *outside* the home.

An empowered woman in the home feels She has the support to speak out in the office and in everyday life. Maybe She won't be harassed (though chances are She will be, at least in more passive ways) but She can feel safe to speak out against it when it happens to other women, as well as be a support system for them because She is confident in herself and knows She has the emotional support of Her most important ally: you.

## Glossary

**Command and Conquer Meeting** - A meeting, usually weekly or bi-weekly where future events are planned and issues discussed. It usually is broken into 4 sections: Planning, Q&A, Safe Space and the Pledge.

**Domination and Submission** - a lifestyle where one member of the household is dominant over the other. The submissive works to serve the needs and demands of their dominant, someone they have agreed to cede power to in return for an abdication of certain responsibilities.

**FemDom -** Femdom is shorthand for 'Female Domination'. This is a sexual style (more than an act, it is often a host of acts) where the Female is the authority and in control of the ways and means of sex.

**Female Dominant Household** - A household where the Female Dominates Her subordinate. This form of domination can take many different forms. In this household the subordinate answers directly to the Female leader and serves Her needs first.

**Female Leadership** - *Female Leadership* is a structure in which the household is built around the control and direction of the dominant woman in the house.

**Getting Things Done** - is a concept surrounding the male ability to accomplish herculean tasks. By providing concrete lists and specific, non-vague tasks, one can tap into men's ability to disconnect the mental and engage in heavy labor for long periods of time with maximum efficiency.

**Her Way** - The idea that in order to best serve a mistress one must commit not only to doing what She desires but performing it in the way She prefers, because for harmony Her way is the best way.

**Her Word is Final** - A critical concept in a Female Dominant household. The idea is to limit conflict and remove unnecessary argument, the submissive male accepts that Her word is final in all serious matters and agrees to support Her decisions, whether he agrees with them or not.

**Natural Authority** - Natural Authority is the inherent ability to lead, combined with an inborn grace that lends an aura of leadership. In women it comes through evolution and design.

**Pledge** - This is an oath made from the submissive to the female leader. It is spoken at the end of the command and conquer meeting and any time the Female Leader may require it, for instance, after a disagreement and reconciliation as a way of putting a bow on the reconciliation. It is an act of submission designed to foster trust, reinforce his desire to serve and Her belief in Her leadership and authority.

It is personal to each couple but should contain the following: A statement of surrender to the Female Leader, referring to Her as a 'natural leader' or having 'natural authority', words of praise and thanks and an expression of Honor, Respect, Devotion and Love.

**Servitude -** The Third and final state in service of a Wife or Girlfriend. A state of submission where the male acts with a commitment to putting Her needs first, committing to doing things Her way and supporting Her decisions with positivity and enthusiasm, even if he disagrees with Her decisions. True servitude cannot be achieved unless he has both surrendered to the idea of Her natural authority and submitted to Her leadership.

**Submission -** It is the second state in service to a Wife or Girlfriend. The action of accepting the authority of the Female leader, characterized by a change in behavior (though not a change in the core being) to better support the needs of the Female leader. Submission involves accepting that Her word is final, Her judgement is best and Her authority is natural. It also involves learning to listen, placing Her needs first, and trusting in Her abilities. I cannot be accomplished without first surrendering to the idea of Female Leadership.

**Surrender** - The first state in service to a Wife or Girlfriend. It is the act of surrendering oneself over to the idea and belief in Female leadership. This is characterized by a husband first accepting his leader's natural authority over him. It is usually formally cemented with a pledge proclaiming his surrender and acquiescence to Her dominion.

# A Note From the Author

Thank you for taking the time to read this far! I hope you found this book informative and helpful to you. If you decide to enact a Female Led household and find success, please reach out to me at keybarrettMSC@gmail.com with the subject line "Commentary". I would love to (Confidentially!) hear how it worked, what worked for you, what didn't. Or feel free to just drop me a line.

If you feel so inclined I would love to interview you both for later editions. It could be your pull quotes in between the chapters (with pseudonyms or not). Thanks again and I wish you the best of luck and the utmost happiness in your newfound respect for each other.

Printed in Great Britain
by Amazon